THE ART OF
NAUSICAÄ
—OF THE VALLEY OF THE WIND—

お前たちの
王は死んだ

From Hayao Miyazaki's concept sketches

About This Book

This collection is made up of concept sketches, cels, film, and key frames for the animated film *Nausicaä of the Valley of the Wind*, created, written, and directed by Hayao Miyazaki. We hope that it serves to deepen the reader's understanding of the world of *Nausicaä of the Valley of the Wind*. Concept art was done by art director Mitsuki Nakamura. Image processing and backgrounds were not done for some cels, and there may be some that differ from those in the actual film.

Index

Hayao Miyazaki Concept Sketches

Hayao Miyazaki drew a number of concept sketches for the film proposals for *Rowlf* and *Sengoku Majo* (Warring States Demon Castle). Shown here are those that most closely resemble images seen in *Nausicaä of the Valley of the Wind*.

風使いの娘ヤヌ

Tapestry

The tapestry used in the background of the credits (handwoven; thick fabric incorporating pictures and designs). Six tapestries were drawn by Miyazaki himself.

Sea of Decay

One thousand years have passed since the collapse of industrial civilization in the great war known as the "Seven Days of Fire," and a massive toxic jungle exuding poisonous vapors covers an earth strewn with rusting ruins; a rotting ocean— the Sea of Decay. The Sea of Decay grows in scale with each passing day, threatening the survival of a weakened humanity. A variety of spore-emitting fungus and plants such as the mushigo palm and the hisokusari thrive in the Sea of Decay, and while strange insects such as Ohms, landgrubs, and hebikera live among them, humans cannot set foot in the area without a mask. The spores emitted by the plants of the Sea of Decay contain a powerful toxin that contaminates normal, healthy creatures and brings about death. The story of *Nausicaä of the Valley of the Wind* begins with a scene in the Sea of Decay, replete with the silence of this death.

1

2

1/Background of a forest swallowed up by the Sea of Decay [Concept art]
2/Forest windmill [Concept art]
3/Fungus ejecting spores [Concept art]
4/Yupa advancing through the spores

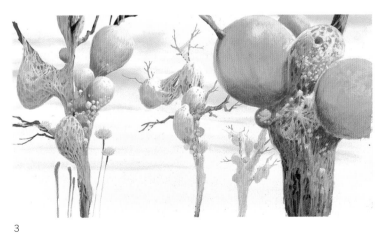

3

4

1–2/Buildings swallowed up by the Sea of Decay [Concept art]
3/Miyazaki concept sketch
4/Yupa wearing an anti-toxin mask [Cel]
5/Room strewn with fungal filaments [Concept art]

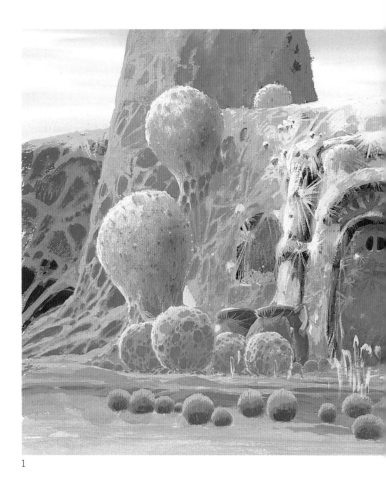

1

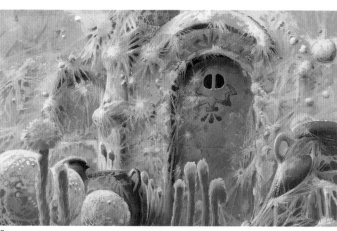

2

3

4

5

1

2

3

4

1

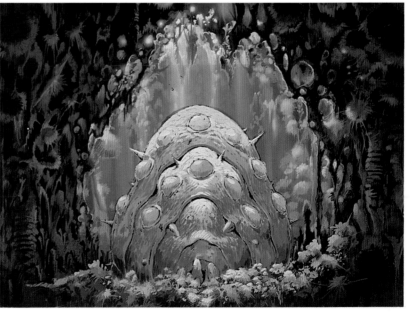

3

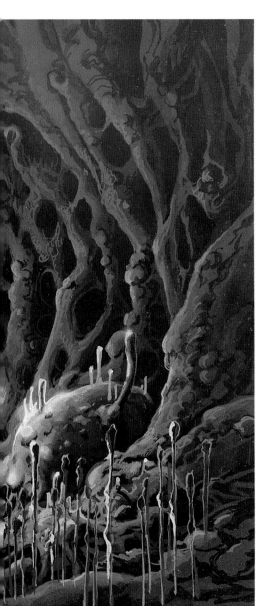

1/Ohm path [Concept art]
2/Ohm path [Miyazaki concept sketch]
3/Ohm shell [Concept art]
4/Ohm shell legs [Concept art]
5/Ohm shell legs

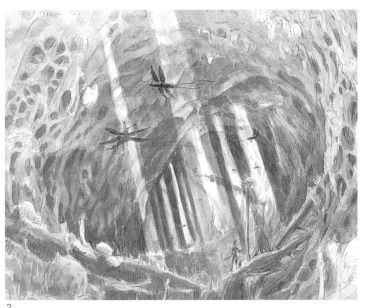

2

4

5

9

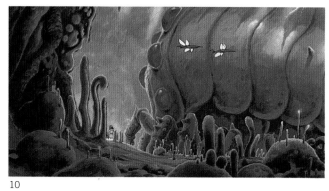

10

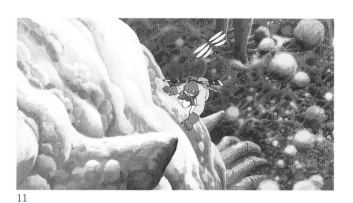

11

12

13

14

15

1/Nausicaä peering into the Sea of Decay [Miyazaki concept sketch]
2–15/The insects of the Sea of Decay

1

1–3/Nausicaä inside the Sea of Decay [Cel]
4/Miyazaki illustration

2

3

1

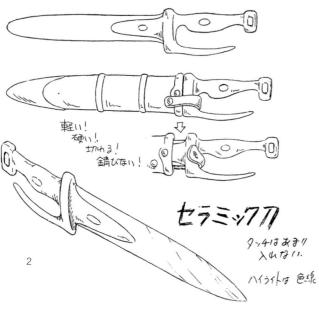

軽い！
硬い！
切れる！
錆びない！

セラミック刀

タッチはあまり
入れない.

ハイライトは 色線

2

3

4

5

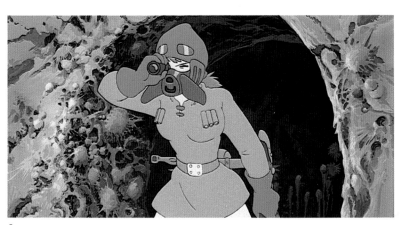

6

1/Nausicaä looking at a ceramic sword [Cel]
2/Ceramic sword design
3–4/Nausicaä sheathing the ceramic sword
5/Anti-toxin mask Nausicaä, Yupa, and horseclaw designs
6/Nausicaä peering through a scope
7/Nausicaä taking a test tube out

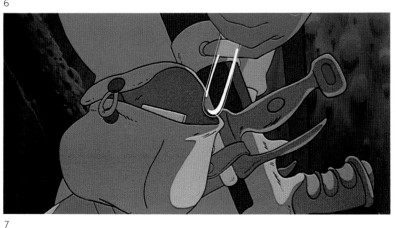

7

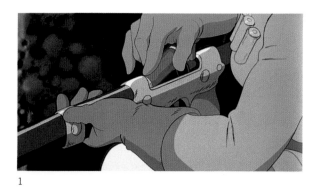

1

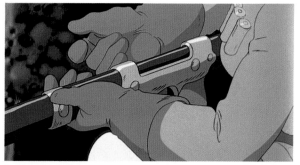

2

3

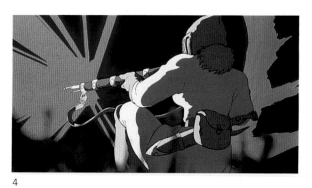

4

5

6

8

9

10

11

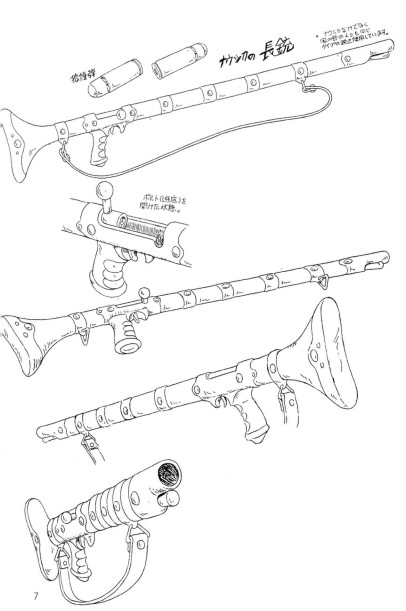

猟爆弾

ナウシカの 長銃

● ナウシカだけでなく
風の谷の人々も同じ
タイプの銃を使用しています。

ボルト（遊底）を
開けた状態。

7

1–2/Loading a siren shell into her rifle
3/Nausicaä readying her rifle [Cel]
4–5/Rifle firing
6/Nausicaä loading a siren shell [Cel]
7/Nausicaä's rifle design
8–11/Nausicaä takes a shell from her chest
and removes the Ohm eye

Desert

A vast desert sits between the Sea of Decay and the Valley of the Wind. It is here that Nausicaä is reunited with Yupa when he is being chased by an Ohm. Anti-insect towers have been built in the desert to prevent the entry of insects from the Sea of Decay into the Valley of the Wind. The windmills attached to the tops of the towers make a curious noise when they spin, keeping the insects away to create a kind of safe zone.

2

1/Petrified Giant Warrior [Concept art]
2/Anti-insect towers [Concept art]
3/Nausicaä flying above the Sea of Decay
[Miyazaki concept sketch]

3

1

2

3

4

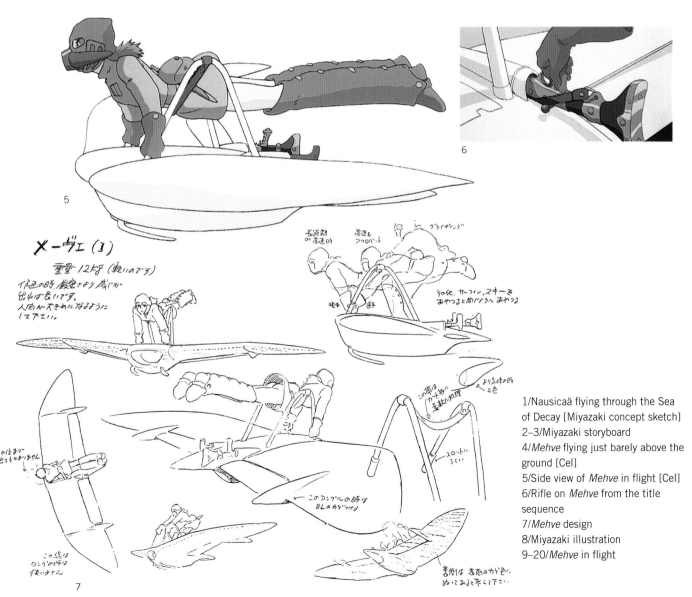

6

5

メーヴェ（１）

重量 12kg（裏いです）

低速の時/最後がより速が
出ればよいです。
人間が大きめに見るように
して下さい。

1/Nausicaä flying through the Sea of Decay [Miyazaki concept sketch]
2–3/Miyazaki storyboard
4/*Mehve* flying just barely above the ground [Cel]
5/Side view of *Mehve* in flight [Cel]
6/Rifle on *Mehve* from the title sequence
7/*Mehve* design
8/Miyazaki illustration
9–20/*Mehve* in flight

7

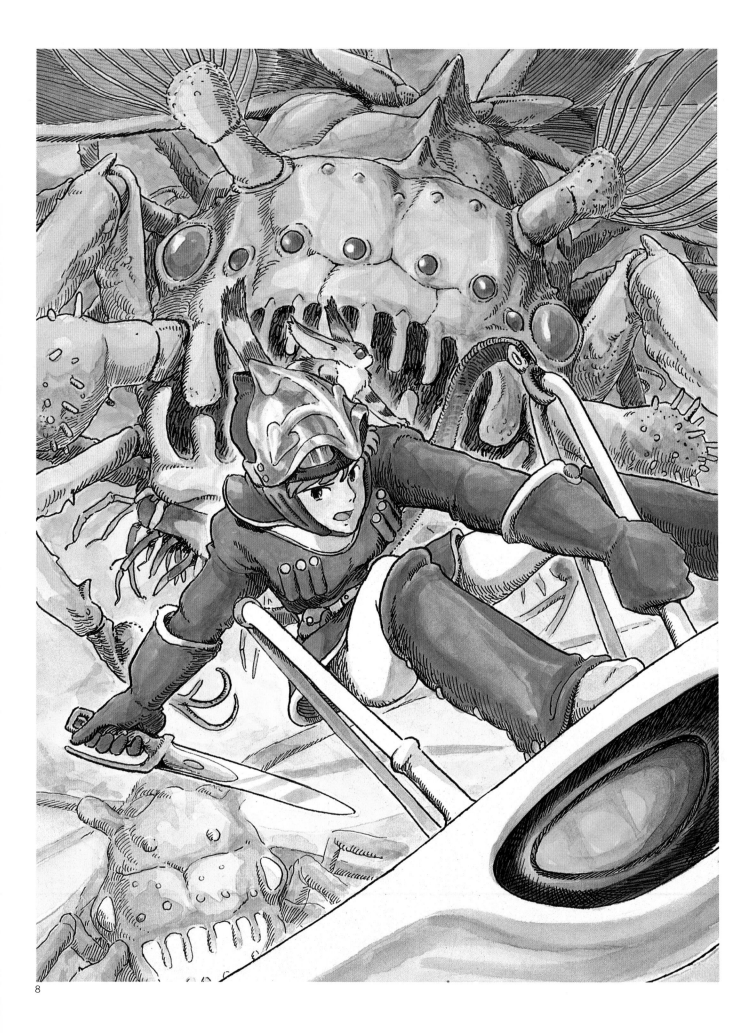

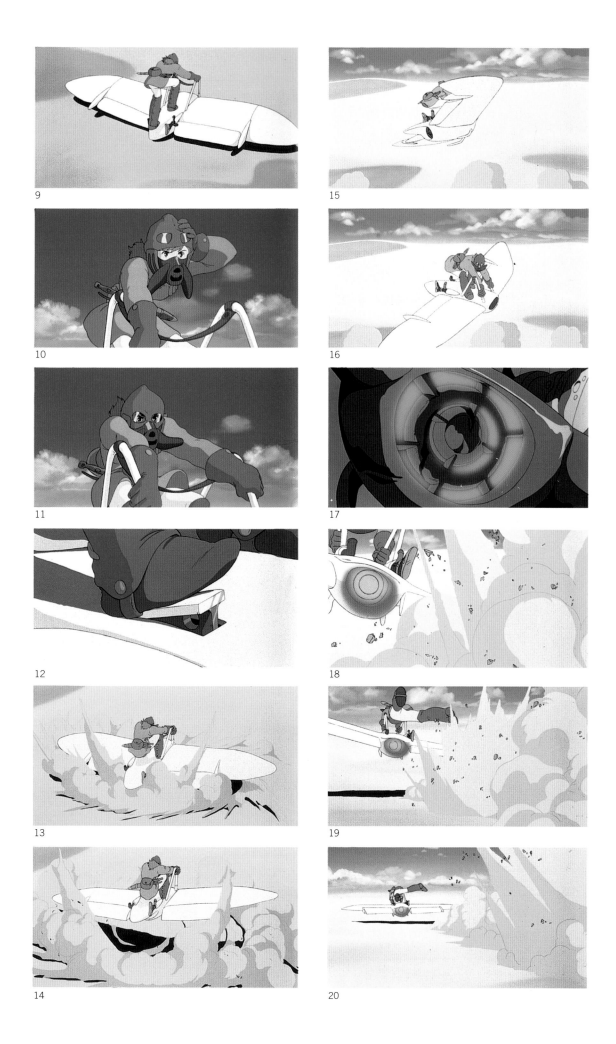

9

10

11

12

13

14

15

16

17

18

19

20

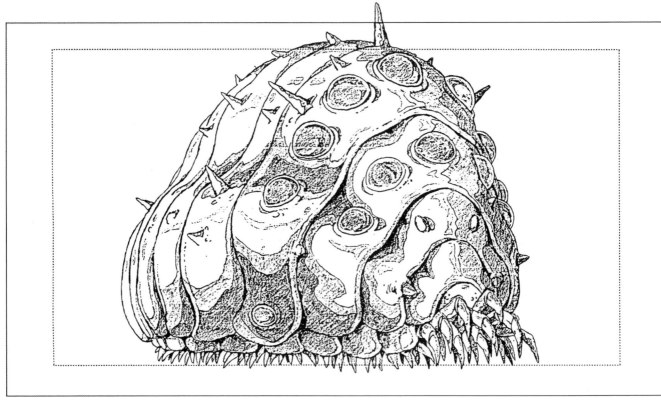

2

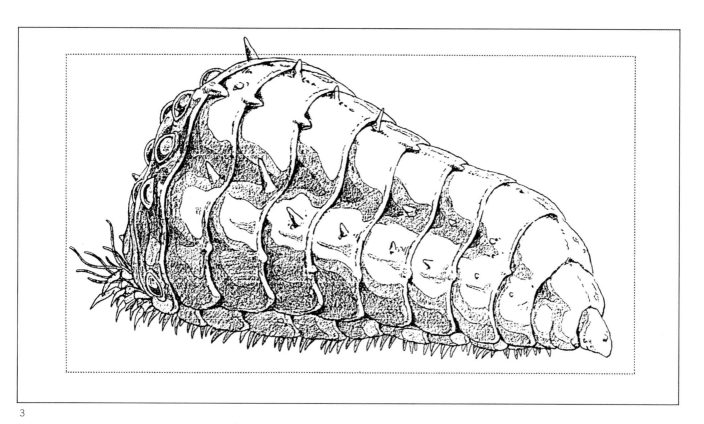

3

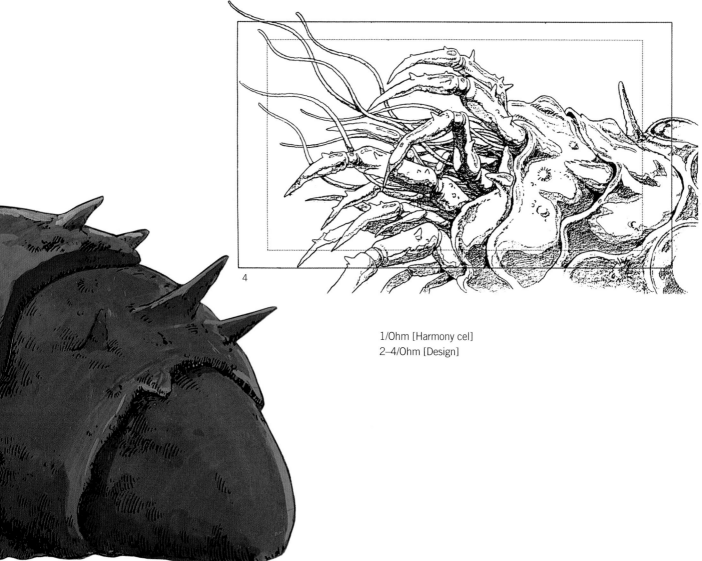

4

1/Ohm [Harmony cel]
2–4/Ohm [Design]

1

1

2

3

4

5

6

1–10/Ohm charging out of the Sea of Decay
11/Angry Ohm [Harmony cel]

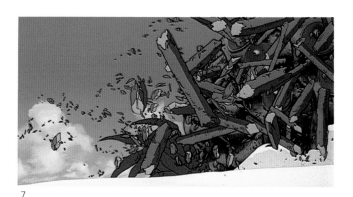

7

8

9

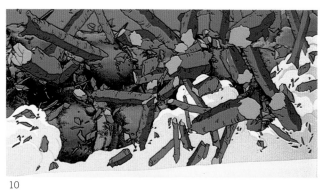

10

11

53

1

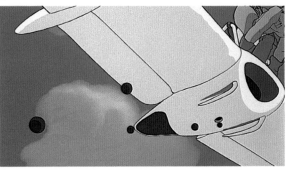

2

3

6

4

1/Ohm closing in on Yupa
2–4/Flare to quell the Ohm's rage
5–6/The motionless Ohm [Cel]
7–10/Nausicaä calming the Ohm with an insect charm

5

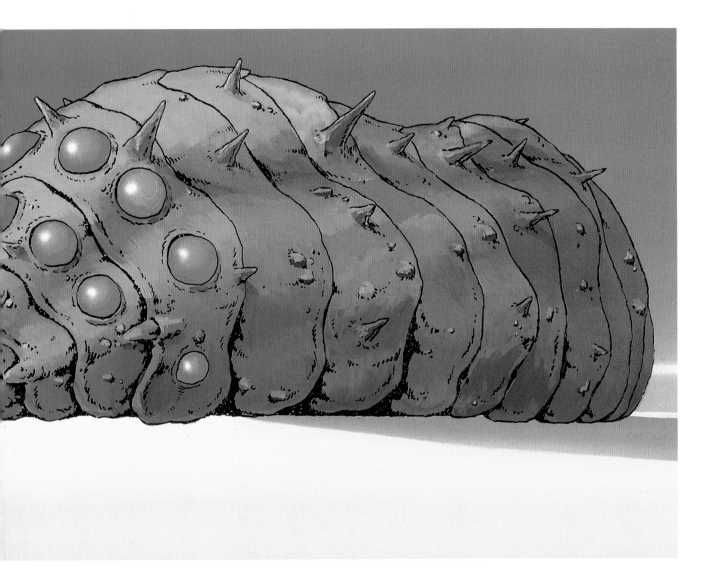

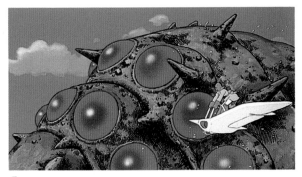

7

8

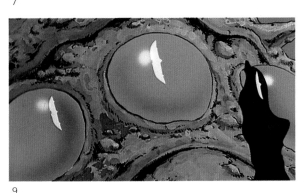

9

10

1–4/Miyazaki illustrations

1

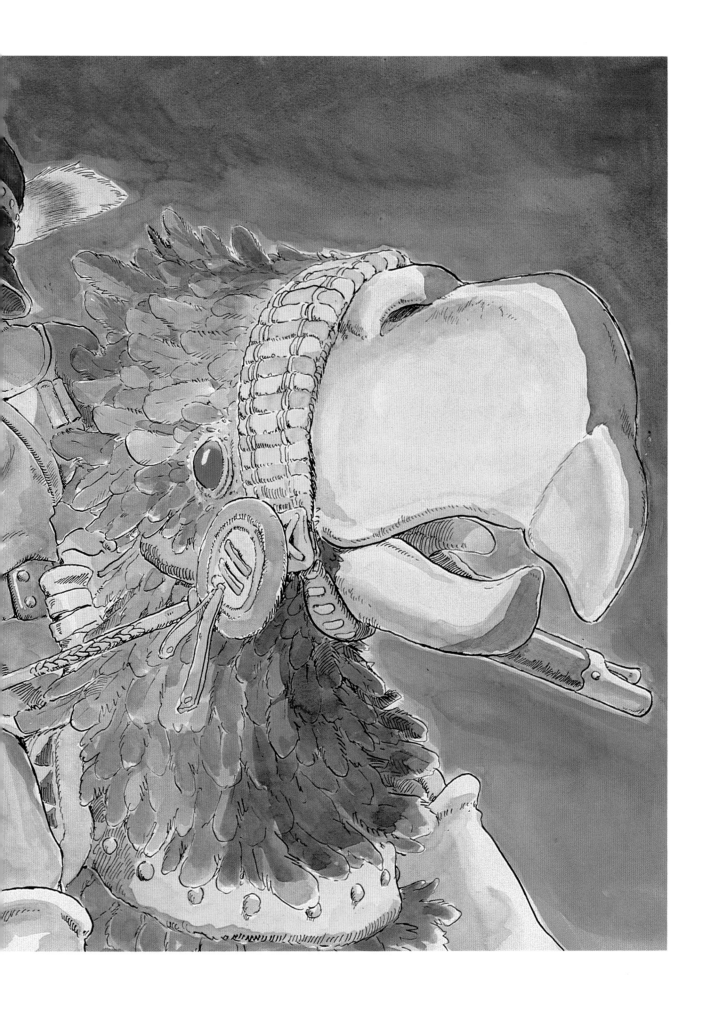

3

4

1

1–3/Nausicaä [Miyazaki concept sketches]
4/Nausicaä on the gunship [Miyazaki concept sketch]
5/Nausicaä [Miyazaki concept sketches]
6/Nausicaä [Design]

ナウシカ
月よく 敏ひうな少女

2

風使いの杖

ハンコーにも

クランクにも
なる
(ヨワ機角へ調整)

フックとなる

3

4

5

1

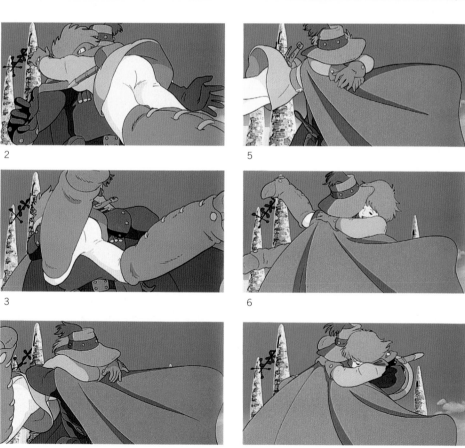

2

5

3

6

4

7

1/Yupa greeting Nausicaä [Cel]
2–7/Yupa and Nausicaä's reunion
8/Yupa [Design]
9/Yupa and Nausicaä [Cel]

8

9

1

2

3

1–3/Miyazaki concept sketches
4/Yupa on his horseclaw [Cel]
5/Horseclaw [Design]
6/Horseclaw [Cel]
7/Nausicaä delighted at being reunited with Kai and Kui [Cel]

4

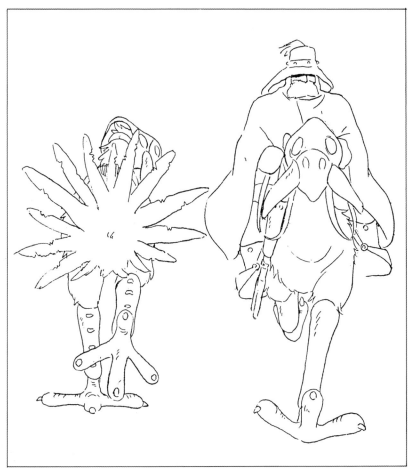

5

6

7

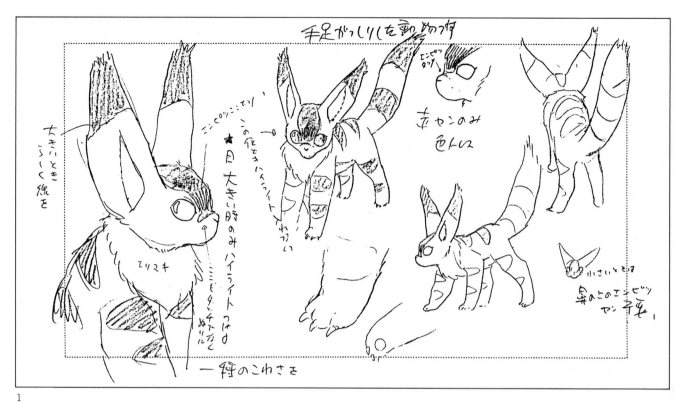

1

2

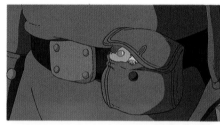

3

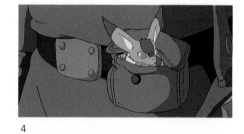

4

5

6

68

7

8

1/Teto [Miyazaki design]
2/Teto [Design]
3–6/Teto poking out of Yupa's pouch [Cels]
7/Teto licking Nausicaä's finger [Cel]
8/Teto and Nausicaä [Miyazaki concept sketch]

The Valley of the Wind

The Valley of the Wind where Nausicaä lives is a small kingdom with a population of a mere five hundred people in a remote region; it just barely manages to avoid harm from the miasma of the Sea of Decay thanks to the wind blowing in off the ocean. Anti-sand slats have also been built at the entrance to the valley to prevent clouds of miasma sand from blowing in. As the name suggests, the wind always blows here, and the people pump water from underground and supply it to the fields using windmills all over the valley and large windmills on the castle, the valley's main feature. The citizens are mainly farmers, coexisting peacefully with the Sea of Decay, and are led by Nausicaä's father, Jihl, who is the tribe chief; the five old men of the castle; and the old woman, Obaba. But they face an unfortunate crisis when the Giant Warrior excavated from beneath the city of Pejite is brought into the valley by the Tolmekian army.

1

1–3/Valley of the Wind
  [Miyazaki concept sketches]

2

1

2

74

1/Valley of the Wind castle [Concept art]
2/Valley of the Wind scene [Concept art]
3/Valley of the Wind bird's-eye view [Concept art]

3

1/Nausicaä and Mito on top of a windmill [Miyazaki concept sketch]
2/Anti-sand slats [Cel]
3–4/Windmills of the Valley of the Wind [Cels]
5–7/People of the Valley of the Wind [Cels]
8/Yupa holding Toeto's child [Cel]
9/Nausicaä and the people of the Valley of the Wind [Cel]
10/Designs for the boys and girls of the Valley of the Wind

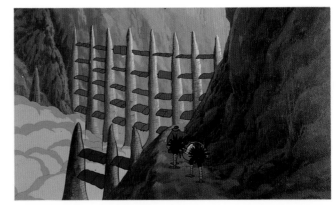

2

3

4

5

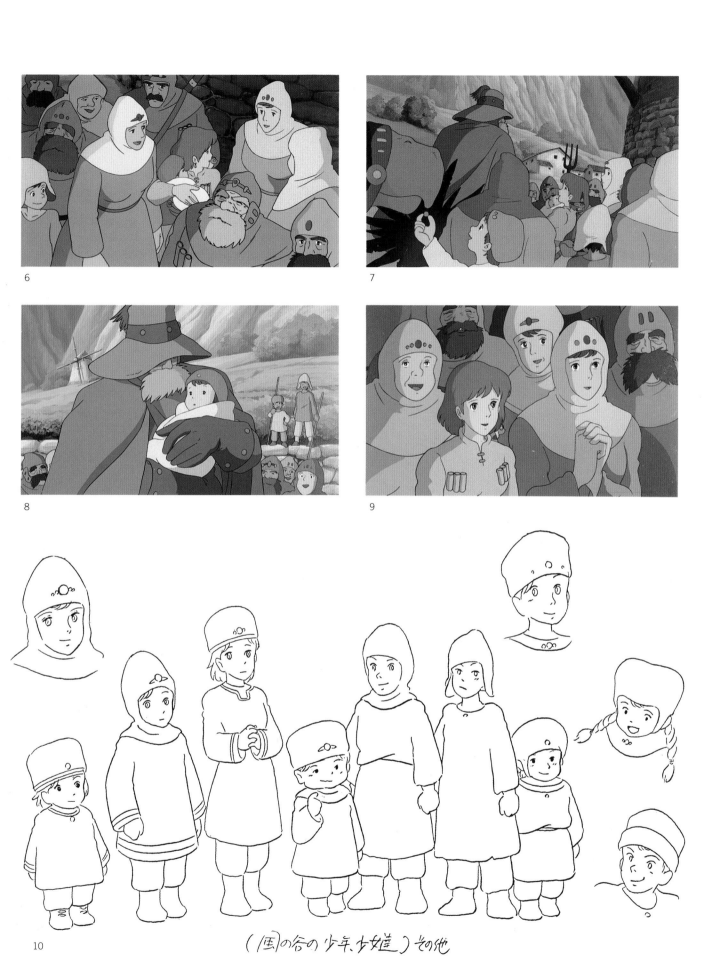

6

7

8

9

10

（国の谷の 少年、少女達）その他

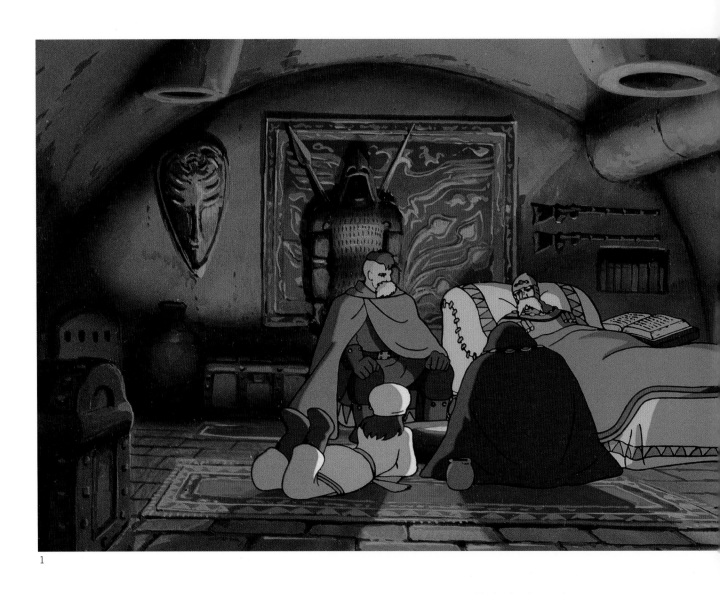

1

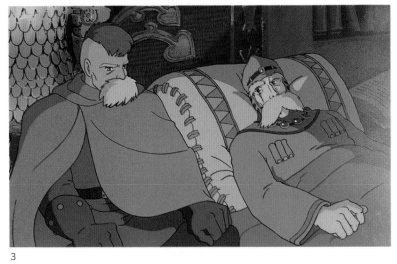

3

2

1/Jihl's room [Cel]
2/Jihl [Design]
3/Jihl and Yupa [Cel]
4/Jihl's room [Concept art]
5/Jihl holding his sword [Cel]

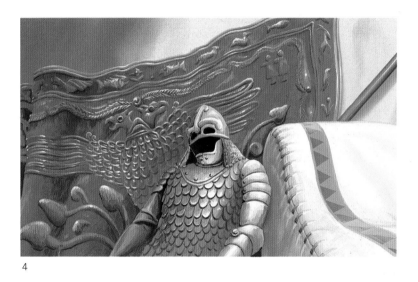

4

5

1

2

1/Obaba and Nausicaä [Cel]
2, 4/Valley of the Wind tapestry [Concept art]
3/Obaba design
5/Nausicaä's ordinary attire [Design]
6/Nausicaä in ordinary attire [Cel]

3

4

5

6

1

1/Lastel through the window [Cel]
2/Lastel [Design]
3–4/Tolmekian Bumblecrow [Harmony cels]
5/Burning ship [Concept art]

2

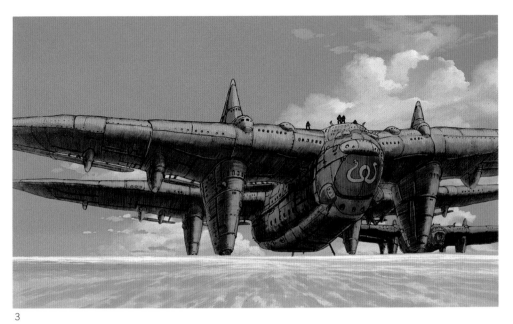

3

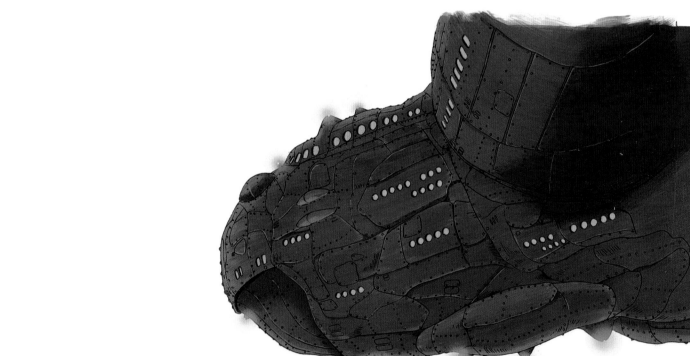

4

5

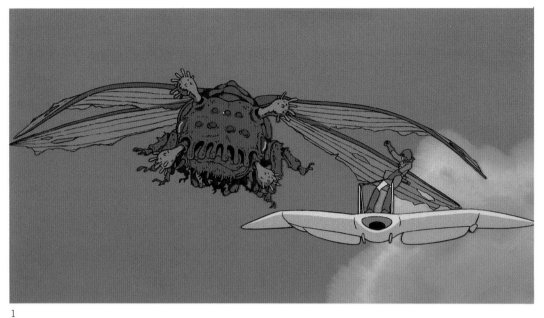

1

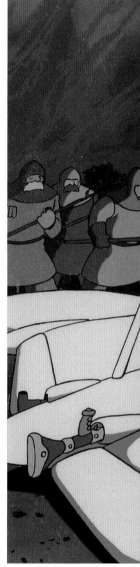

4

2

1/Nausicaä leading the Ushiabu [Cel]
2–3/Ushiabu [Cels]
4/Nausicaä spinning insect charm in front of the Ushiabu [Cel]
5/Ushiabu [Design]

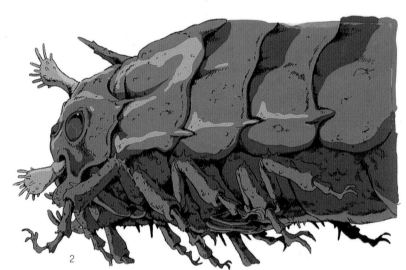

3

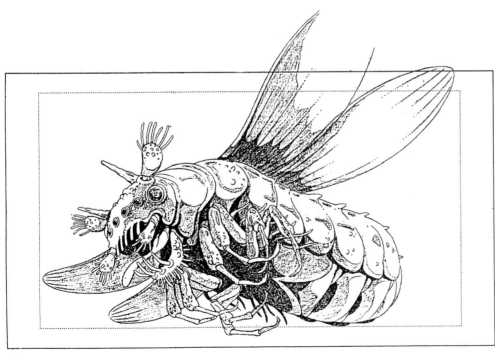

5

1

1/Bumblecrow formation [Harmony cel]
2/Korvet cutting in front of a Bumblecrow
3–4/Bumblecrows entering the Valley of the Wind
5/Bumblecrow [Miyazaki concept sketch]
6, 8, 11, 12/Bumblecrow [Cels]
7/Bumblecrow cockpit
9/Bumblecrow gun turret
10/Bumblecrow jet
13/Bumblecrow [Design]

2

3

4

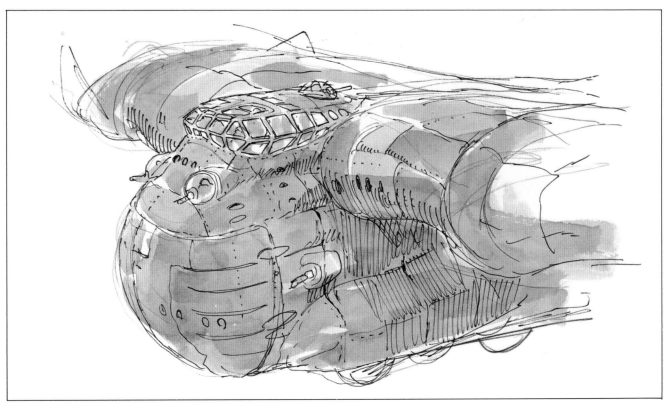

5

6

7

8

9

10

11

12

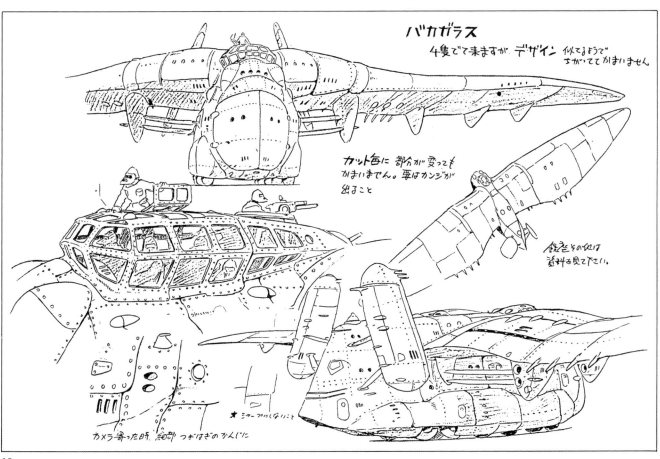

バカガラス

4隻で出て来ますが、デザイン 似てるようで
ちがってて かまいません

カット毎に 部分が 変っても
かまいません。要は カンジが
出ること

細部etcの仕げは
資料を見て下さい。

★ シャープにしないこと

カメラ寄った時、細部 つぎはぎの かんじに

13

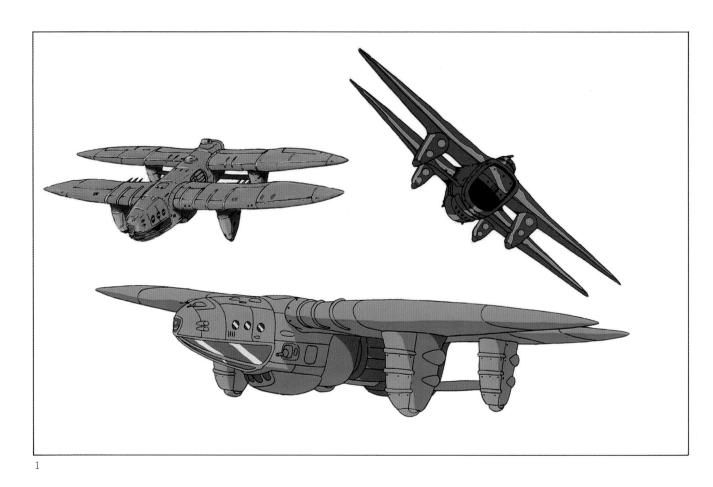

1

2

3

1/Korvet [Cel]
2/Korvet and Bumblecrow pre-departure
3/Korvet seen from the Brig cockpit
4/Korvet gun turret
5/Korvet [Design]
6/Korvet [Cel]
7/Scene with 6 in use

4

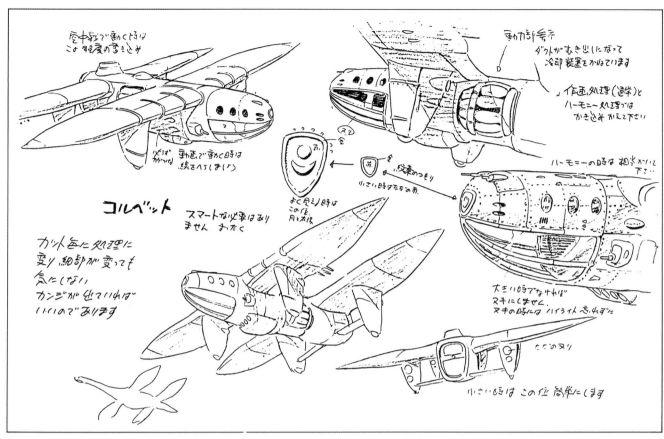

5

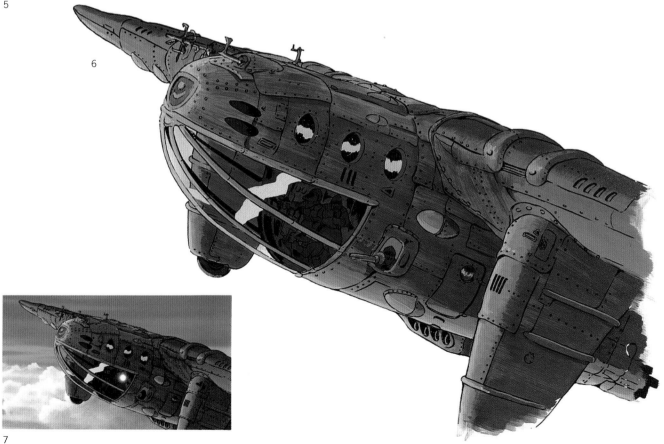

6

7

1

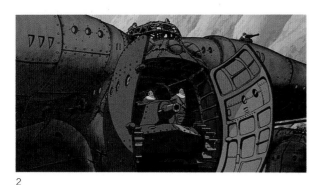

2

3

4

1, 6, 7/Tolmekian tank stolen by the old men of the castle [Cel]
2/Tank exiting the Bumblecrow
3/Tank side view
4/Tanks lined up [Cel]
5/Tank [Design]
8/Tank firing

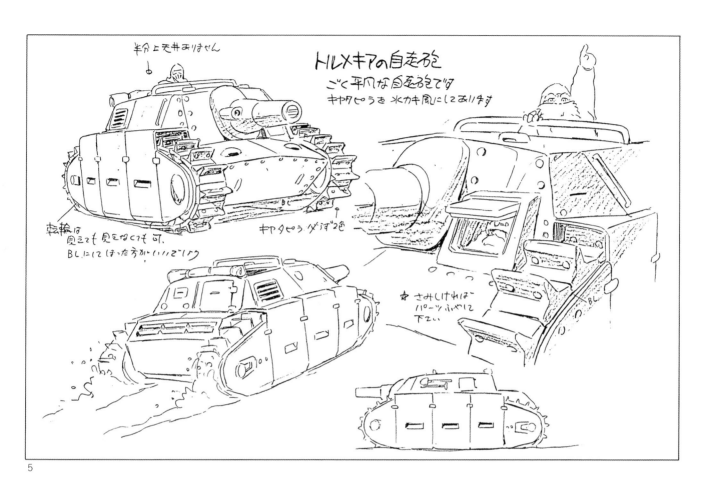

5

6

7

8

1

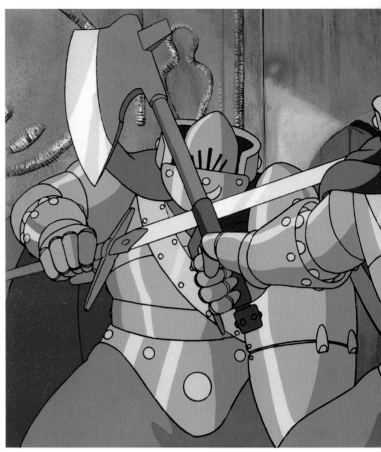

2

3

4

1/Tolmekian soldier [Designs]
2, 3, 8, 9/Armored warriors [Cel]
4/Ship soldier [Cel]
5–6/Command soldiers
7/Armored soldiers [Miyazaki concept sketch]

7

5

8

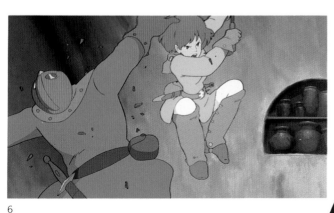

6

9

1

2

3

4

5

6

1/Kushana [Miyazaki illustration]
2, 6/Kushana and Kurotowa [Cels]
3–4/Kushana [Cels]
5/Kushana uniform [Design]
7/Kurotowa [Design]
8–13/Kurotowa [Cels]

7

8

9

10

11

12

13

1

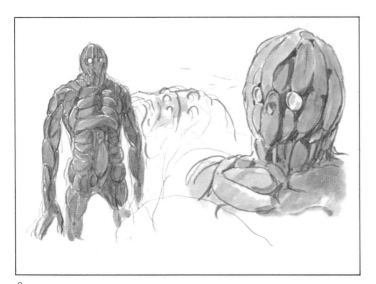

2

3

4

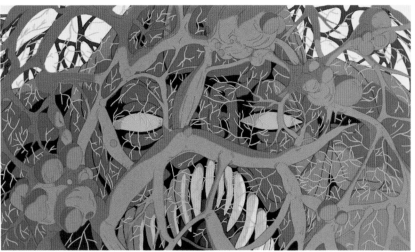

5

1/Giant Warrior [Cel]
2/Giant Warrior [Miyazaki concept sketch]
3/Opening credits storyboard
4–5/Giant Warrior embryo being cultivated [Cels]
6/Giant Warrior cultivation device [Concept art]

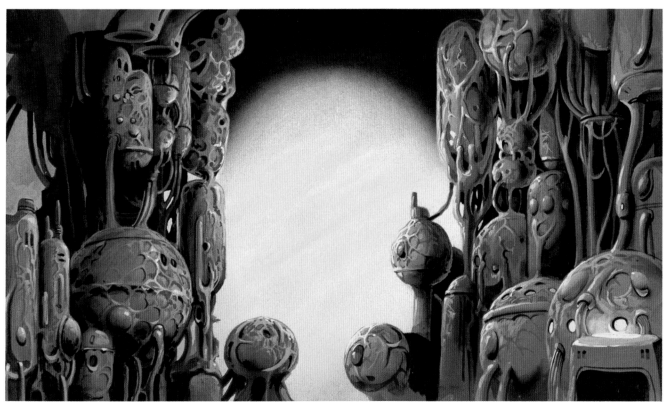

6

1

2

3

4

5

6

7

8

1/Secret room [Concept art]
2/Secret room [Miyazaki illustration]
3/Secret room [Cel]
4/Teto [Cel]
5/Chiko nut girls
6/Nausicaä accepting the chiko nuts from the girls [Cel]
7/Obaba and the chiko nut girls on the scrapped ship [Cel]
8/People of the Valley of the Wind on the scrapped ship [Cel]

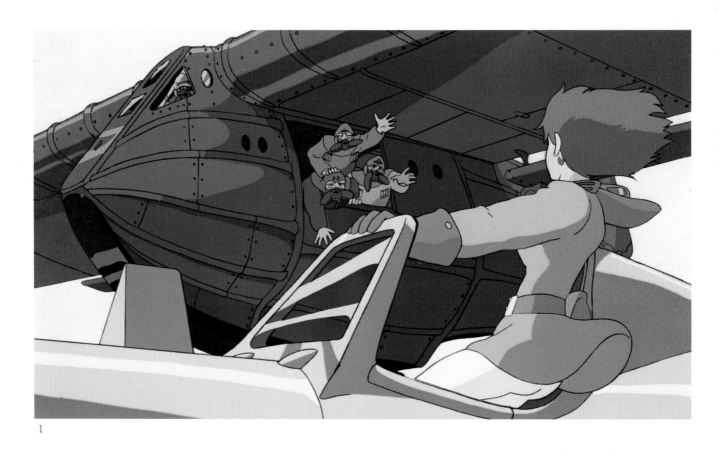

1

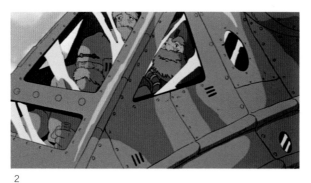

2

3

4

5

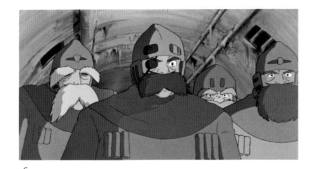

6

1/Barge and gunship [Cel]
2–5/Barge
6/The old men of the castle with Mito at the center [Cel]
7–12/Old men of the castle designs
13/Gol, Niga, and Gikkuri [Cel]

7

8

9

10

11

12

13

The Bottom of the
Sea of Decay

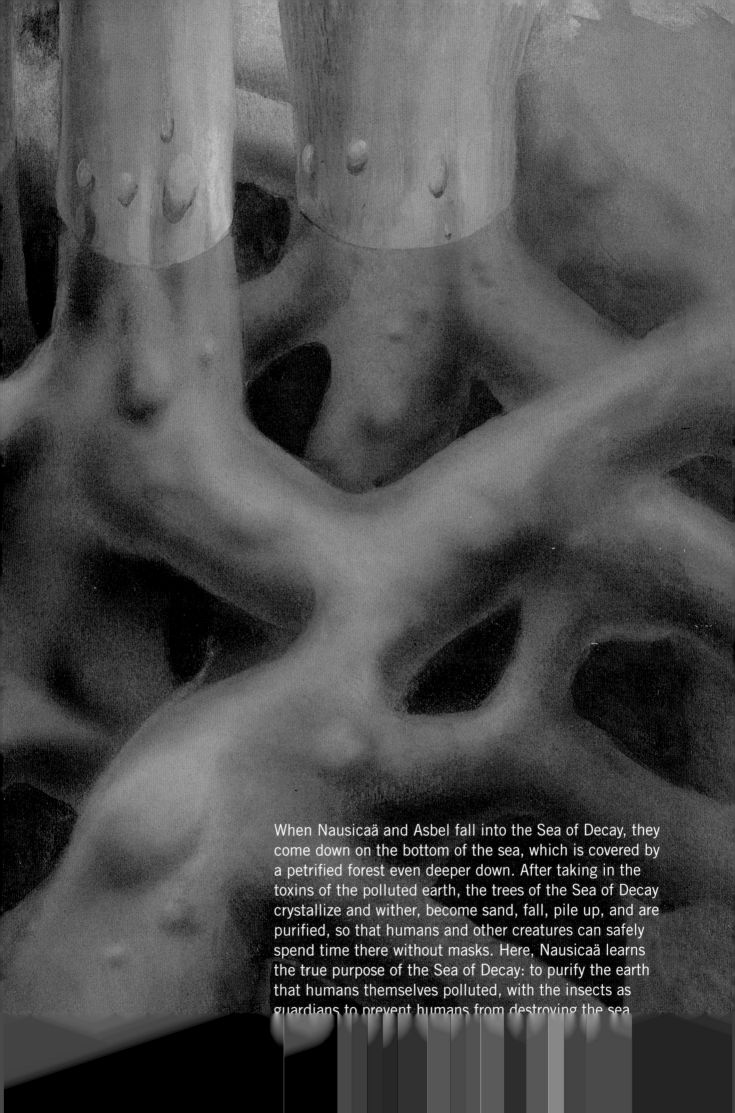

When Nausicaä and Asbel fall into the Sea of Decay, they come down on the bottom of the sea, which is covered by a petrified forest even deeper down. After taking in the toxins of the polluted earth, the trees of the Sea of Decay crystallize and wither, become sand, fall, pile up, and are purified, so that humans and other creatures can safely spend time there without masks. Here, Nausicaä learns the true purpose of the Sea of Decay: to purify the earth that humans themselves polluted, with the insects as guardians to prevent humans from destroying the sea.

1

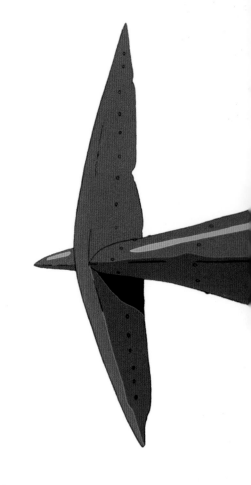

2

3

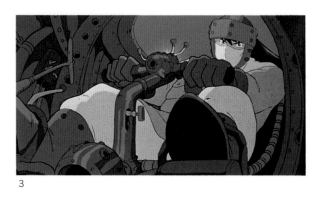

4

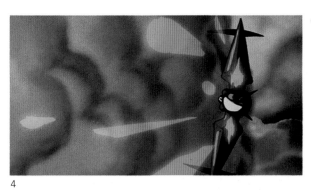

5

1–5/Asbel and gunship
6–8/Asbel and gunship [Cels]

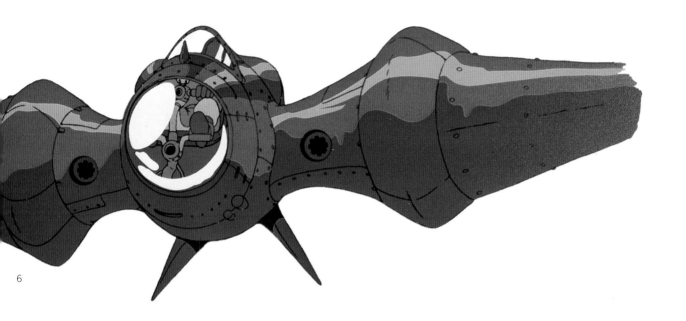

6

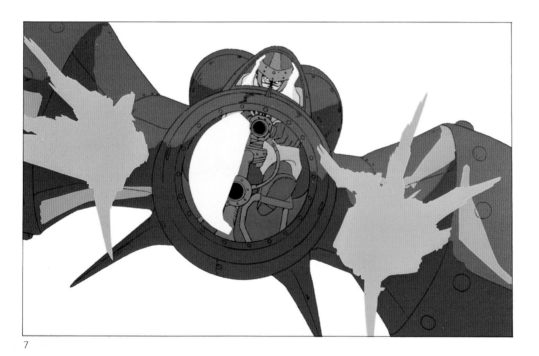

7

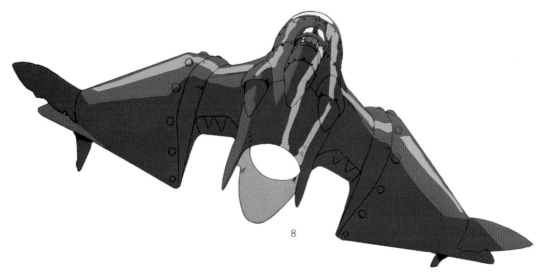

8

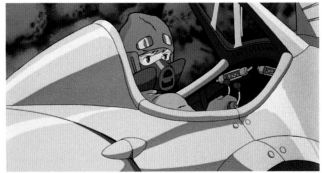

1

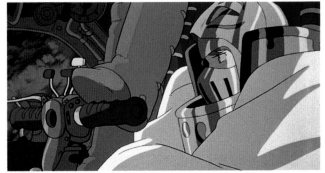

2

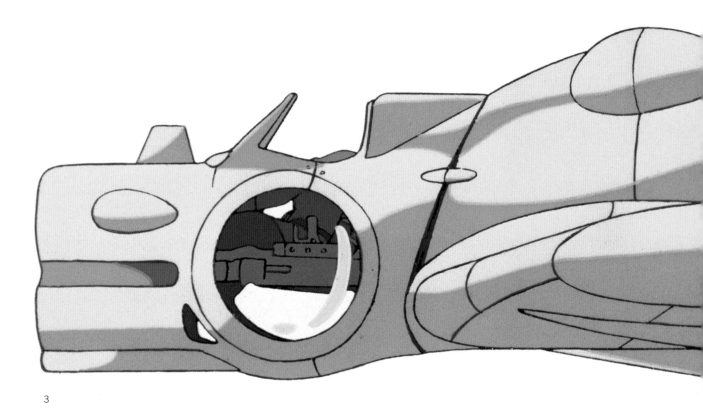

3

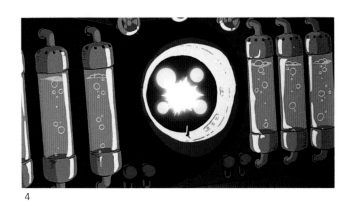

4

5

6

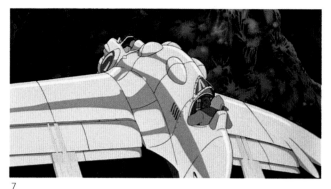

7

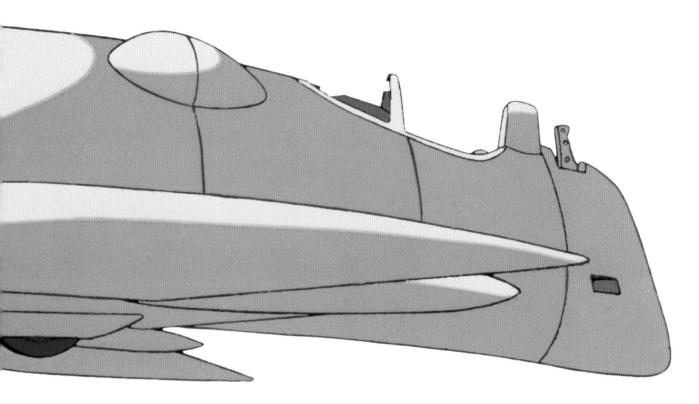

8

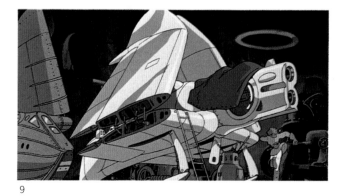

9

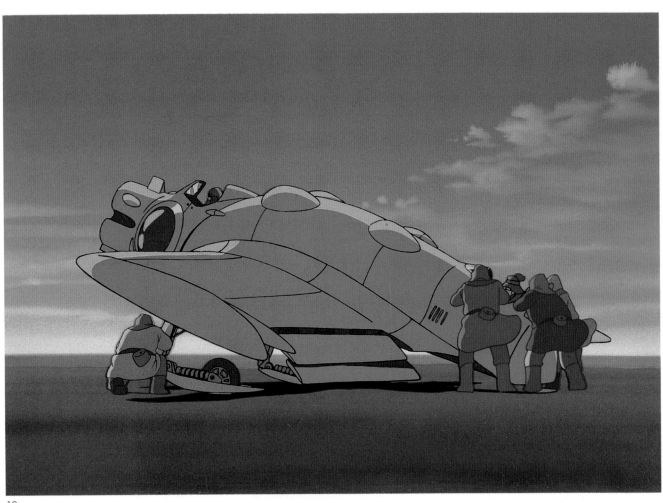

10

11

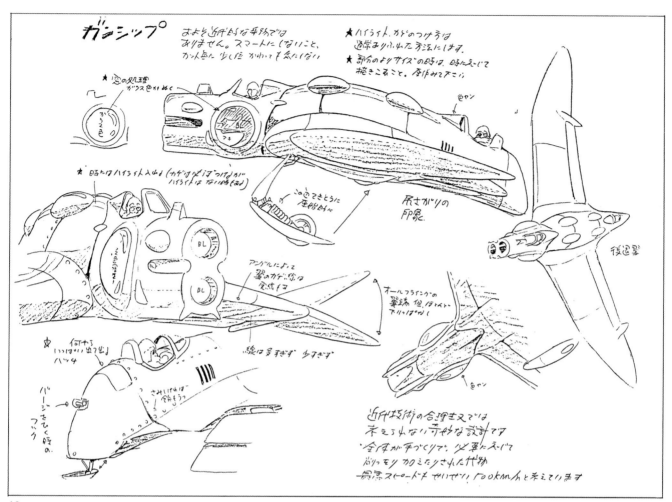

ガンシップ

12

13

1/Gunship front seat
2/Cockpit interior
3/Gunship side [Cel]
4/Gunship instrument panel
5/Rear seat
6/Legs for water and ground landings
7/Gunship rear
8/Gunship firing guns
9/Gunship in castle hangar
10/Gunship taking off [Cel]
11/Nausicaä posing on top of the gunship [Cel]
12/Gunship [Design]
13/Gunship [Miyazaki concept sketch]

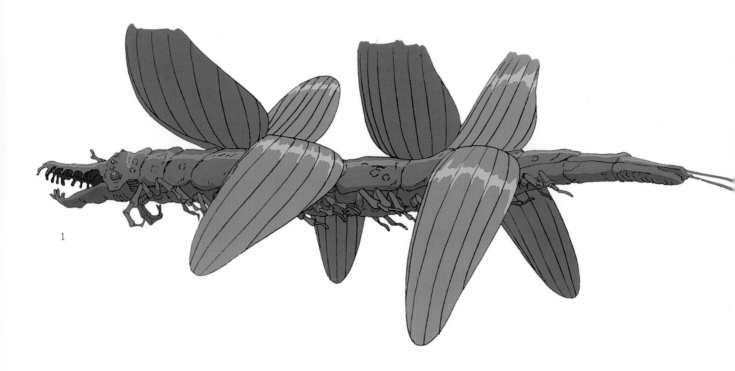

1

2

3

4

1/Royal Yamma [Cel]
2–3/Royal Yamma swarm
4/Sea of Decay [Concept art]
5/Nausicaä [Cel]
6–7/Landgrubs
8/Hebikera
9/Hebikera [Cel]

5

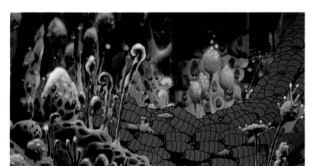

6

7

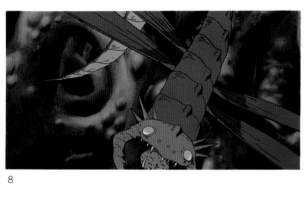

8

9

1

2

3

4

5

6

1–3/At the bottom of the Sea of Decay [Concept art]
4/Nausicaä as a child [Miyazaki illustration]
5–7/Nausicaä as a child [Miyazaki concept sketches]
8/Nausicaä's mother [Cel]
9–11/Nausicaä as a child [Cels]

7

8

9

10

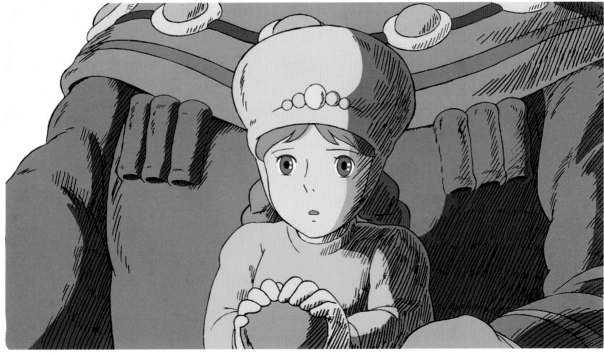

11

1

2

3

4

1/Nausicaä and Teto [Miyazaki illustration]
2/Asbel [Miyazaki concept sketches]
3–4/Asbel [Cels]

Pejite

Pejite is a city of artisans separated from the Sea of Decay by a massive mountain range. Under the leadership of their mayor, the people are possessed by the powerful desire to burn the Sea of Decay and take back the world for humans. Thus, when they happen to discover a "Giant Warrior," one of the monsters of the old world, they try to revive it. But after they are overcome by the border guards of the powerful military state of Tolmekia, the citizens are forced to abandon the city. With their little remaining fighting power, they send in rampaging Ohm to confront the Giant Warrior, slaughtering the Tolmekian forces stationed in the city, before bringing danger to the Valley of the Wind as well.

1/Nausicaä and Asbel on their way to Pejite [Cel]
2, 4, 6/Pejite [Miyazaki concept sketches]
3/Pejite overview [Concept art]
5/Inside Pejite [Concept art]

1

2

3

ペジテ、崩壊した宇宙船を寄生する町。

4

5

ペジテ

6

1

2

1/Brig [Cel]
2–3/Inside the Brig [Concept art]
4/Brig from above
5/Korvet on the Brig
6/Brig from below
7/Room where Nausicaä is confined
8/Brig cockpit
9/Brig [Cel]

3

4

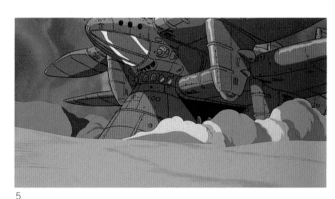

5

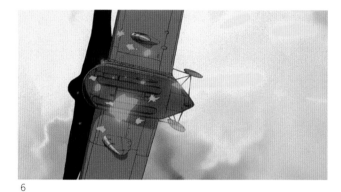

6

7

8

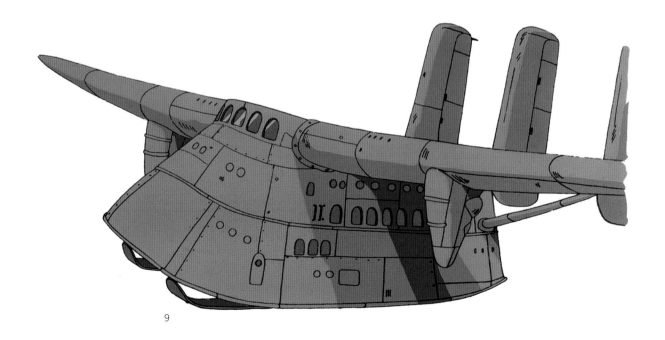

9

1

3

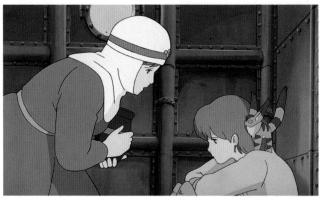

2

4

1/Lastel's mother [Cel]
2/Nausicaä's would-be double [Cel]
3/Lastel's mother talking to Nausicaä [Cel]
4/Double removing her clothes [Cel]
5–6/The people of Pejite

5

6

Acid Lake

Acid Lake sits in one corner of the desert, near the anti-insect towers. Affected by the miasma of the Sea of Decay, the water is strongly acidic; simply touching it will cause serious injury. It is on a sandbar of this lake that Nausicaä saves the baby Ohm. Also in the area are the remains of a spaceship that traveled between the stars before the Seven Days of Fire. Fighting the Tolmekian army, the people of the Valley of the Wind barricade themselves in this wreck and wait for Nausicaä's return. This is where the story of *Nausicaä of the Valley of the Wind* comes to an end.

1

1–5/Scrapped ship at Acid Lake [Concept art]
6/Chiko nut girls standing on the ship

2

3

4

5

6

1

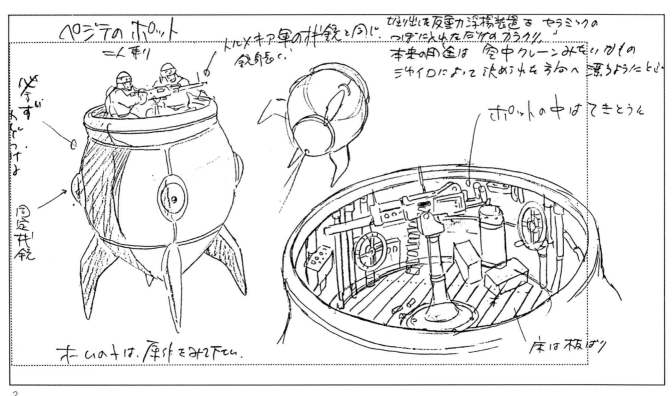

2

3

4

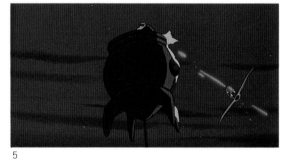

5

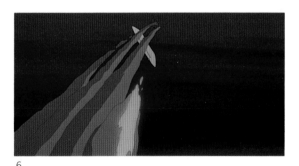

6

7

8

1/Miyazaki concept sketch
2/Flying pot [Miyazaki design]
3/Nausicaä on *Mehve* [Cel]
4–8/Flying pod [Details]

1

2

3

4

1/Nausicaä with the flying pod machine gun [Miyazaki illustration]
2/Nausicaä waiting for the herd of Ohms [Cel]
3/Nausicaä injured
4/Nausicaä pushing back the baby Ohm as it moves toward the lake [Cel]
5/Nausicaä crying [Cel]

5

1

2

1/Kushana ordering the mobilization of the Giant Warrior [Cel]
2/Giant Warrior and tank
3–4/Giant Warrior [Original sketches]
▶1–24/Giant Warrior moving

4

3

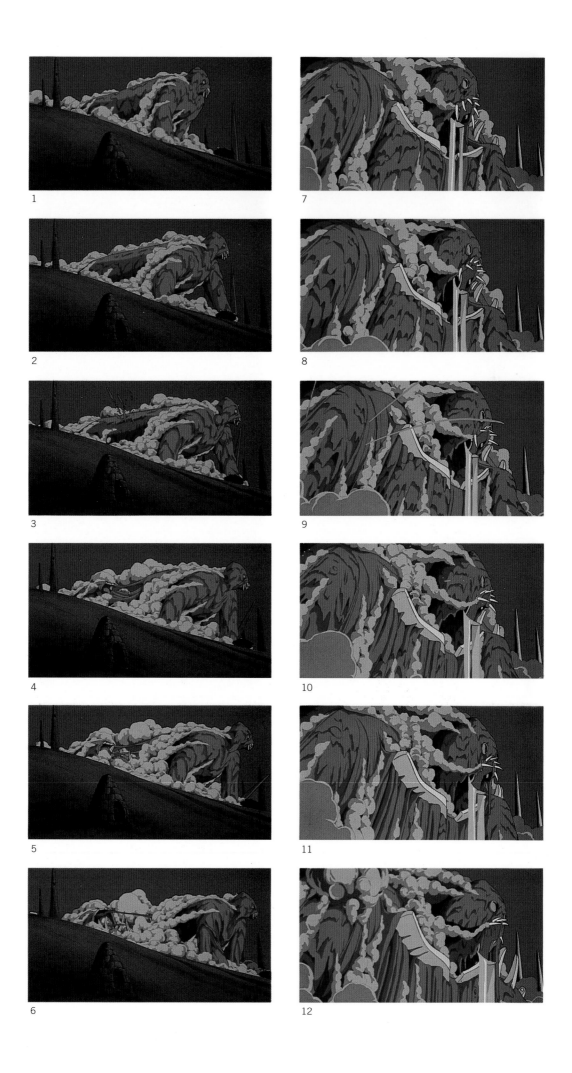

1

2

3

4

5

6

7

8

9

10

11

12

13

14

15

16

17

18

19

20

21

22

23

24

1

2

3

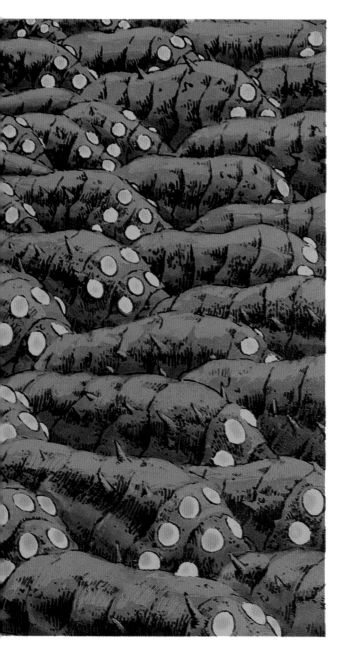

4

5

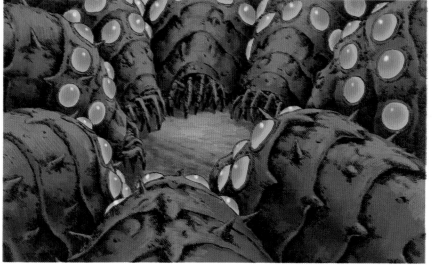

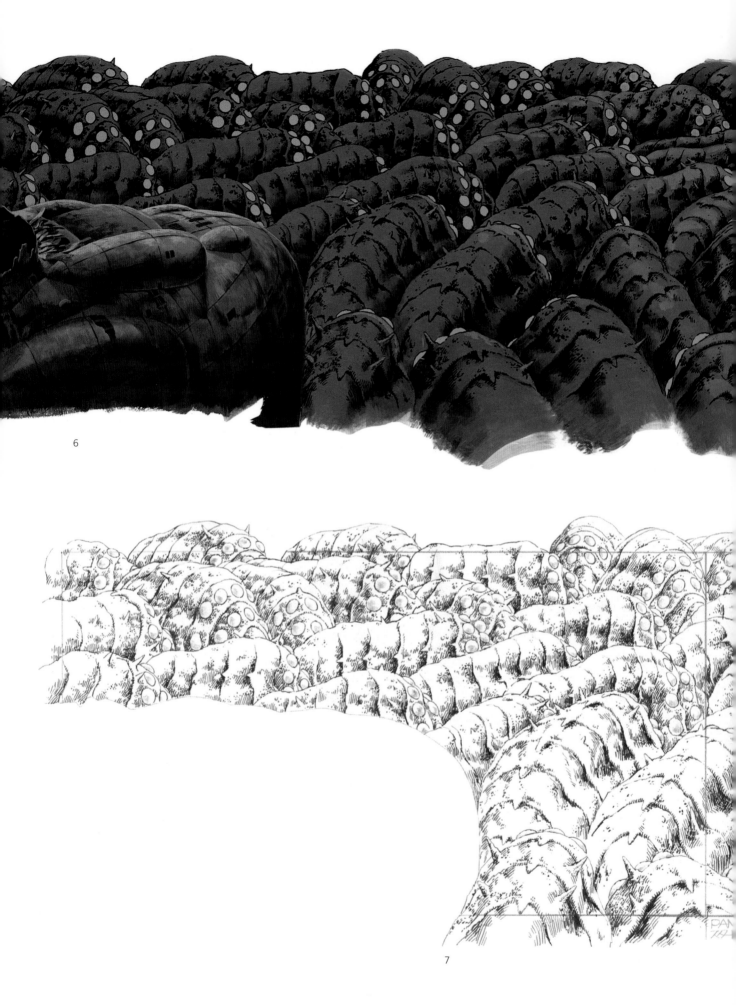

6

7

1–3/Ohm [Harmony cel]
4/Advancing Ohms
5–6/Ohm herd surrounding the injured Nausicaä [Harmony cel]
7/Original sketch of 6
8/Ohms [Original sketch]

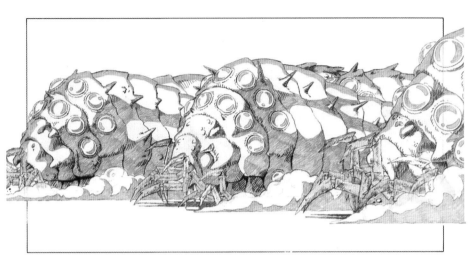

8

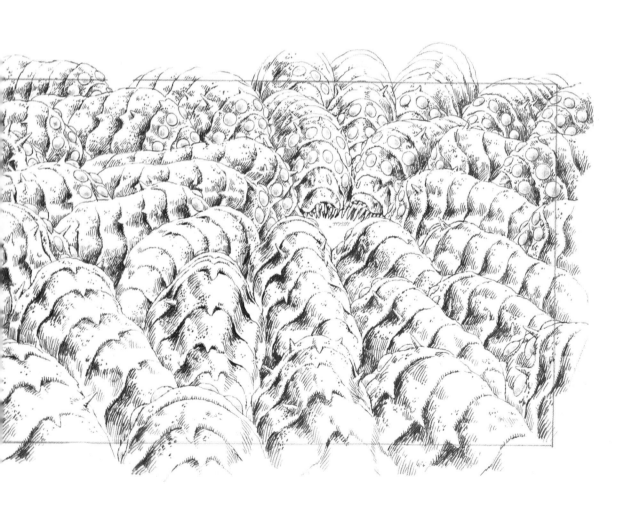

1

2

148

1/Smiling Nausicaä [Cel]
2/Nausicaä waking up [Cel]
3/Messenger in the blue robes [Cel]
4/Nausicaä smiling gently [Cel]

3

4

Animation Technique
in *Nausicaä of the Valley of the Wind*

Hayao Miyazaki explaining the Ohm multiplane setup to Sumi Shimamoto, who played Nausicaä.

Text and Layout: Kazuyoshi Katayama

Introduction

Normally, even the briefest explanation of animation techniques would fill an entire book. Thus, given the page constraints and nature of this collection, I decided it was essentially impossible to give readers a comprehensive overview of the basics of animation techniques *and* discuss *Nausicaä*, so instead, I will give an abbreviated summary of the techniques used. Rather than taking a top-heavy approach, the goal of this section is to allow an insight into the process through the use of selected stills and accompanying captions; basically, "to get *this* shot, you do *this*."

Vocabulary

- **Panning:** Move the direction of the lens with the camera position fixed. "Pan down" is moving the camera down, "pan up" is turning it upward.
- **Move:** Film while moving the camera position.
- **Follow-pan:** Keep the target in the center of the field of view and follow its movement by panning. The camera is fixed.
- **Follow:** Keep a target in the center of the field of view and follow its movement by moving the camera.
- **Dolly in:** Film while moving the camera forward. One type of move.
- **Dolly out:** Method of filming moving the camera backward.
- **Multi:** Abbreviation of multiplane. Filming on an animation stand with multiple levels. The focus is on one part of the screen.
- **Total multi:** Multi using a pan-focus on the entire screen.
- **Wraparound:** Nickname. Fix the camera above a moving target and follow-pan.
- **Fr.In (frame in):** Japanese-English term to indicate that the target enters the center of the camera frame.
- **Fr.Out (frame out):** Conversely, the target leaves the camera frame.
- **Overlap:** Method of shifting to a new shot bit by bit, double-exposing the end of the shot and the beginning of the next, doubling the images.

(Excerpted from the commentary of the animation book *Horus no Eiso Hyogen* by Isao Takahata)

Kazuyoshi Katayama

Born August 28, 1959, in Kyoto. After leaving Telecom, he worked as a production assistant for the first time on *Nausicaä of the Valley of the Wind*.

Special Effects

We didn't create a special camera system specifically for the film *Nausicaä of the Valley of the Wind*. All the effects were produced by making imaginative use of existing devices and readily obtainable materials. The director ordered the staff to specially develop the three techniques introduced here, given that they were to depict key scenes in the movie, and we succeeded in producing truly marvelous results. I wouldn't hesitate to call all three techniques "special effects."

P.D

Sea of Decay spores (transmitted light)

The spores dance bewitchingly at the bottom of the Sea of Decay like fireflies, almost as though they were alive. The truth behind this movement is transmitted light. Normally, transmitted light is a type of double exposure, so after filming the background and the cel, you wind back the film and shine light on the former and film it. However, in this shot, to depict the light of the spores themselves and the light around them, we had to film it twice for one spore. In other words, to shoot the movement of one spore, the film was wound back two times. Incidentally, there are seven spores in this cut. If they all appeared at the same time, it could have been filmed a total of three times, but that's not how it went. That sort of unnatural movement would never happen. The seven spores were all filmed with their own individual timing, and there were even some with the light enhanced or weakened with fades in or out, so to shoot this one shot, the film had to actually be wound back fourteen times and was filmed a total of fifteen times. Because this takes far too much time and labor, this method was not used for any shots besides this one.

Ohm Multi

Animation is not good for depicting the scale and weight of the Ohm. The multi device came from the idea of possibly making the pieces of the Ohm move separately with something like paper cutout animation.

Naturally, there is a way to move several objects on an animation stand rather than animating them, for whatever reason (it's called total multi). But given that the limit with that method is, at best, five or six pieces, and we would be moving a dozen Ohm body parts at different speeds (timing), that was definitely not going to work. Thus, we were faced with the need to develop a device to make this possible. What came out of the brainstorming was an idea applying the basic principle of a bellows. We connected the Ohm's body

with a flexible material, and by expanding and contracting this material, we increased and decreased the gaps between the pieces. Essentially, we could make it look like the Ohm's entire body was expanding and contracting. Not only that, but the difference in the contraction and expansion for points near where force was applied (the speed) was large and became smaller farther out on the body. It was actually the ideal technique.

We selected sewing elastic for the connecting material, and that choice was absolutely perfect. The device was later called the "elastic multi" by the staff and was improved upon in a variety of ways until it was perfected.

One of the many elastic multi prototypes made during the development process. The shell that makes up the Ohm is a harmony treatment, painted from the back of the cel using paints just like a normal animation cel. But it's colored with an essentially pictorial method and is positioned between the animation cel and the background. In *Nausicaä*, groups of planes and (part of) the Giant Warriors, among other things, were also depicted this way, to create a presence with real impact.

Elastic Multi Construction

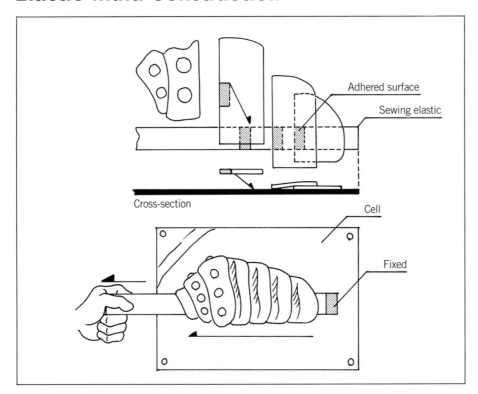

Adhered surface

Sewing elastic

Cross-section

Cell

Fixed

The pieces of the Ohm shell (cel) are attached to the elastic so that they're always overlapping as in the diagram. The Ohm with the elastic is then attached to the cel in that direction, completing the device. This device is affixed to the animation stand, and then the remaining elastic is fixed to a different stand and moved (pulled). This is the structure of the elastic multi.

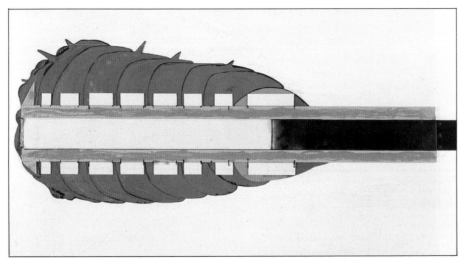

One of the elastic multis used in this film, a type with the elastic attached to the center of the Ohm body. Stretching out from behind is not elastic, but rather a strip of PVC. This is on top of the same line as the elastic and connected with the elastic. In other words, when this strip is pulled, the elastic stretches. But it's always out of the frame and doesn't show up onscreen even if there's a mistake. The white object in the middle of the device is the elastic. This is firmly braced on either side by rails. Even further out are the guides; the former keeps the elastic moving in the same direction, while the latter was thought up to make sure the Ohm shell moves smoothly without any jerking.

2

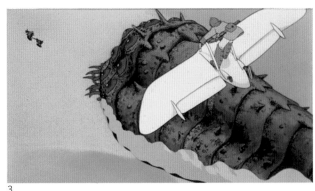
3

4

(1) An example of the simplest use of the elastic multi. In
this shot, the Ohm is just stretched out, so it's hard to see the
effect, but if you look at the sequence of stills, it's obvious.
(2) Shot of the Ohm cutting across the screen. It's made to cut
across the screen by sliding the entire device, and the elastic is
pulled right up to the end.
(3) Similar to (2), the device itself is repeatedly expanded and
contracted, and the entire thing is slid in the direction of the
follow. With the background follow, the sliding device, and the
contraction and expansion of the elastic, this shot took the most
effort to film.
(4) It looks like it's just repeated expansion and contraction
on the spot for the follow shot, but the device is waving to the
sides—albeit very slightly—in this shot while the elastic is
expanded and contracted. (This is repeated with the sliding.)
There are also elastic multis that move up and down (photo on
page 153).

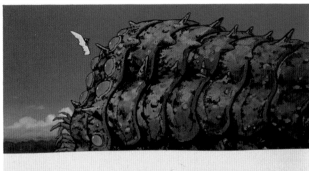
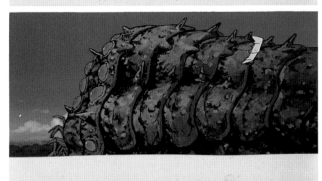
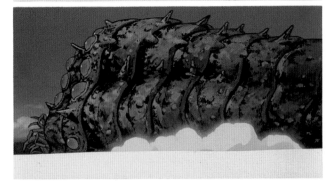
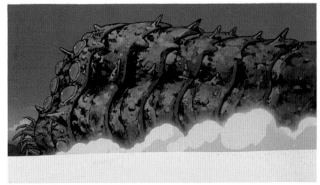
1

Reminiscing scenes

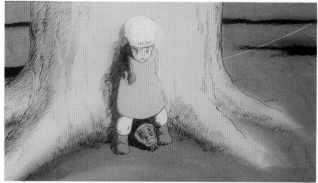

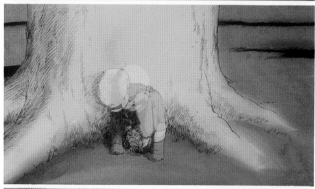

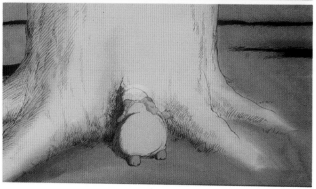

Nausicaä's dream is filled with an afterglow shadowed by painful, sad memories, a double movement almost like a spell on the character. We used a variety of tricks to portray these kinds of unusual scenes.

The screen dyed with the light of the dusk was produced by shining a light from behind the background colored with ink on tracing paper (transmitted light). Also, in this scene, in order to have the overall image be constantly in motion, the background was divided up into the animation of the machine-drawn lines alone, and the tracing paper with the color alone.

Then, with the movement of the character, we aimed for a kind of strobe effect. We exposed the action in one shot one-third at a time, dividing the filming into three parts, but at the time, the action in each individual frame was slightly different and filmed so that it looks like movement in the movie. In other words, to complete one shot, we needed to do three overlaps. We then used a diffusion filter on the finished animation and infused the entire image with transmitted light to complete the effect.

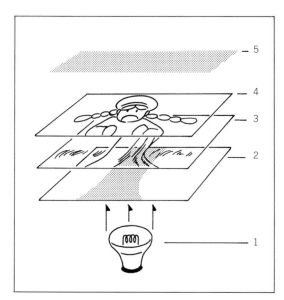

Filming method
1. Light source (transmitted light)
2. Background A (tracing paper)
3. Background B (cel, machine-drawn line alone)
4. Character (cel)
5. Diffusion filter

The transmitted light here is not a double exposure, but is instead a method that uses light as one element of the background. Strictly speaking, it can't be called transmitted light.

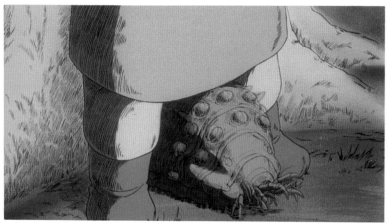

There are the following two types of backgrounds colored on tracing paper.
(Top) A single color for a background with no material effect such as the sky. However, there are several types of single colors.
(Bottom) Colored to match the lines of the cell background.

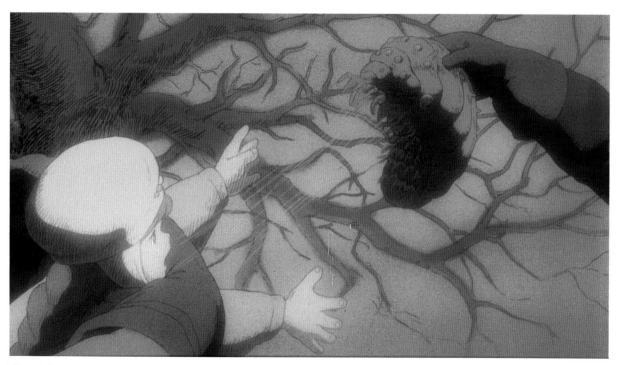

When doing a dolly out to a larger, more disconnected frame than the standard, transmitted light can't be used for reasons to do with the animation stand. Thus, the color tones overall are different from other cuts.

Camerawork

There are a number of different types of camerawork, such as fix, pan, follow, dolly in, and dolly out, but in fact, these techniques are often used in films in combination like follow-pan or dolly in while panning. Here, we'll introduce special combinations of techniques like this. Also, while it's not directly connected with camerawork, we'll spend a significant part of this section on a method called "sliding" that was used a great deal in the film.

Sliding

Sliding was originally developed as a conventional method in limited animation such as TV to cut back on the number of pictures that had to be drawn. Sliding is when a character's cel is pulled according to the animation style, in a method similar to when the background is pulled across the animation stand when following rather than making the characters move. This not only cuts back on the number of images required, but is also used to move characters with multiple multis that can't be animated (the harmonied Ohm and Bumblecrow, etc.) or book cels. The biggest reason we started using it is the first reason I gave. But why do these shots have a power that goes beyond the standard animation?

This is because of the detailed calculations that go into the timing of the slide. You don't simply pull; only when you start to make the same calculations as during animating will the shot succeed. Another reason is that by separating the moving parts from the immobile main body and sliding them together (e.g., the movement of the main body of the gunship and the flaps), the simple movement of the main body is hidden. In other words, in a certain sense, sliding produces the same effect as animating everything, through the calculations when designing the slide of the main body and the animation of the separate parts. The combination of sliding and animating produces the maximum result with the minimum materials; it is an ideal animation technique.

Rolling (to make it look as though the character is flying)

To give a sense of the character's buoyancy when following a flying object cruising through the sky, simply move the character up and down by sliding the character's cel just a little as shown in the diagram. This technique can also be applied to ships and other things. Although it's a simple, it's actually not used very much.

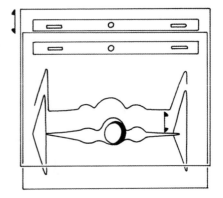

Rolling can be done in the same way, but the impression varies widely depending on the character.
(Top) The stability from the high speed and the lightness of *Mehve* come through quite clearly.
(Bottom) An example of the scope of the rolling made larger, and the powerful impact when used with a group.

The Exquisiteness of Animation + Sliding

1. A "curved slide." Compared with sliding along a single line, an incredible amount of work is required to move a character by sliding them along a parabola. 2. The main body of the gunship braking suddenly with reverse thrusters is slid, while the flaps and the thrusters are a separate animation. If the sliding is not carefully calculated, it is easily beaten by even poor animation. Animation is calculation.

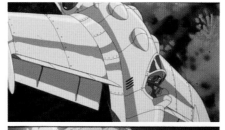

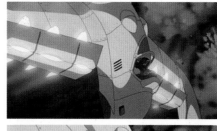

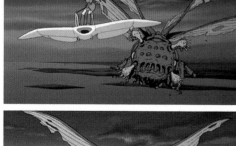

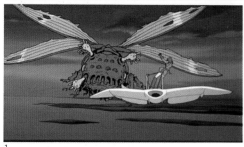

1

2

3

This shot has the Ohm rising up through sliding together with the cel for the water streaming down its body sliding at the same time. For the combination of the Ohm and the water, it goes without saying that because the Ohm surfacing, the waves rising up on the water's surface, and the shadow in the water must all be aligned, this shot required detailed calculations for the sliding and the animation be determined at the original art production stage.

Rotating slide

Just as the name suggests, this method moves a rotating character by sliding. A fulcrum is set up outside the filmed frame, and the character is rotated with that as the center. To explain using this shot of a giant tree as an example, the trunk of the tree and the branches of the upper layers were created separately. By slowly rotating the branches and leaves section (2) sandwiched between the trunk (1) and the background (3), we can depict the swaying of a tree seen from below. In this case, the center that (2) is rotated on is basically in the center of the screen, but it is always hidden under the trunk.

The light shining through the branches is transmitted light; it comes through pinholes in the background rather than any special processing. When (2) is rotated on top of that, the light appears and disappears when it passes through the branches and leaves, so that the entire effect looks like light flickering through a treetop.

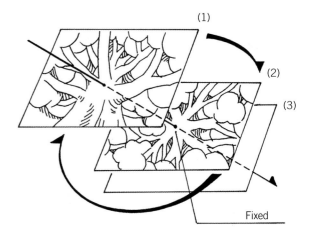

The stills to the left are both examples of sliding with the center of rotation outside the frame.
(Top) The large windmill cutting in front of Nausicaä's room.
(Bottom) The control tower of the scrapped ship being destroyed.

Telescopic effect

This is an attempt to realize with cel animation (on a plane) the effect that can be seen in photography with a telephoto lens. When such a lens is used, the subject does not change in size even if it is advancing toward the camera, so the characters here are moved using sliding. The tanks and the horseclaw are examples of this.

The horseclaw and the last tank in the line are slid below the book cel (the ground in front) to bring them up. In particular, in the shot with the tanks, the key was how to arrange the tanks and set their individual speeds; if they had been even a little off, it would have been a disaster.

An example of where the telescopic effect works best is the opening of *The Castle of Cagliostro*.

Also, rippled glass was used in the tank shot. This was basically to produce a haziness, and this material is essential for producing a telescopic effect.

1

2

Total Multi

This is done with the same sliding, but the effect is a little different.

Animation with normal sliding allows free movement within the frame, but with the total multi, the character is always positioned in the middle of the screen. Only part of the character moves.

Split up into several parts in advance, a character is layered up, and its movement is depicted by sliding these individually at different speeds to depict the movement of a character of multiple materials or to give the scene depth. (1) is the former, while (2) is the latter.

(1) Ohm body rising up.
(2) While minute sliding of the several parts of the machine gun produces a sense of adjusting the sight, it also gives the gun body a nice depth.

Follow

Pan

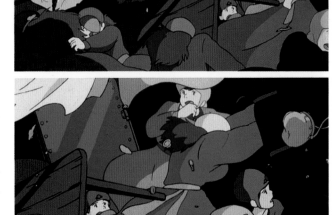

As an example, we'll introduce here shots that bring depth to the screen with a total multi while following and show the character and the world.

(1) Nausicaä walking through the Sea of Decay. The blurry plants in the foreground are gondola, not total multi.

(2) Gunship dropping beneath the clouds.

(3) Nausicaä walking along the bottom of the Sea of Decay. Here, we used tricks to increase the depth of the screen, sliding not only the rows of pillars, but the light shining down from above as a book cel (airbrush).

1

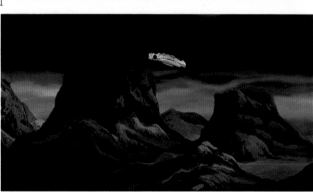

2

3

4

5

Shots with combined camerawork, and not just pan shaking the camera.

(4) Panning right and lift, dolly in and pan, and dolly out are repeated to produce the sense of being inside the ship rocked by turbulence.

(5) Pan/dolly in on the room seen through Yupa's eyes. Actual human eyes don't dolly in, but in this case, rapidly approaching the target gives the viewer the impression of discovery.

Follow Pan

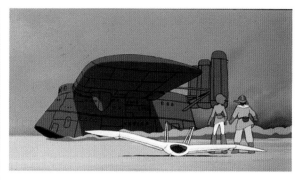

(1) Follow-pan of the Brig. This shot could be said to be typical of follow-panning a target coming from the background.

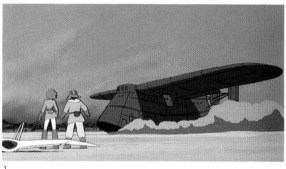

1

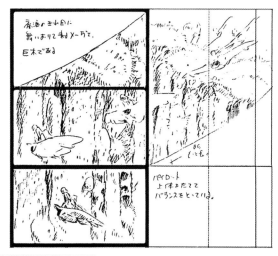

(2) This shot is a follow-pan of *Mehve* coming down a little from above the trees of the Sea of Decay, and what should be noted here is the way of looking at the background accompanying the follow-pan. Notice that the angle of the trees seen from an elevated angle at the start changes significantly with the movement of the camera.

With live action, all you would have to do is move the camera, but that won't work in animation. Everything has to be drawn. Because the relationship between the object of the follow-pan and the background is important, the animator requires detailed calculations from the background art design stage. In other words, the camerawork must have already been decided on at this stage. In this sense, the animator is both a performer and a cameraman.

2

Crane Up

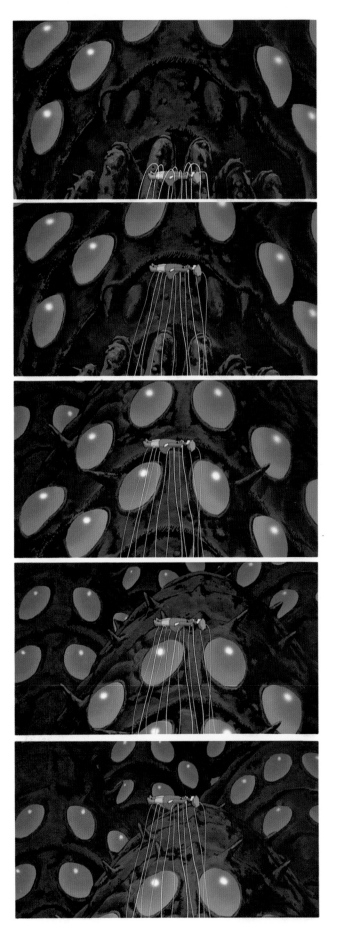

A crane shot is originally a shot filmed in live-action with both the camera and cameraman set on a crane and moved up and down. Here, the camera moves to follow as Nausicaä is lifted by the tentacles and shifts into a crane up, capturing the herd of Ohm. To make this kind of crane shot, the herd was divided into three sections as in the diagram below, and filming was done while sliding a total multi in the direction indicated in the diagram.

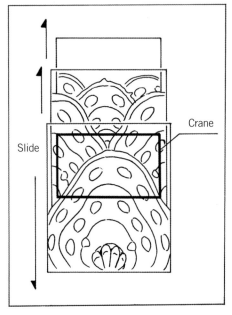

Gondola

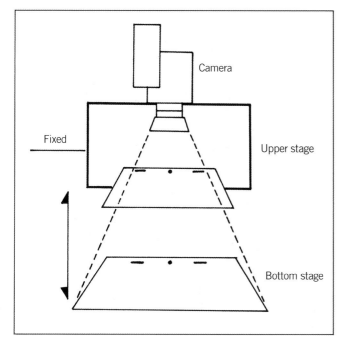

A gondola is a method of filming that uses the animation stand as in the diagram.

The upper stage cel and camera position are fixed and do not change, but movement up and down is possible between this and the lower stage. In this case, the camera focus is only on one stage or the other. Shown here are examples that have the focus on the lower stage.

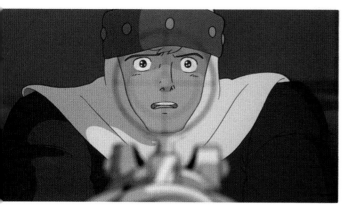

he crosshairs of an anti-aircraft gun.

The Brig's cockpit is gondola.

Flowing clouds 10K with fade out.

Korvet, slide in.

Black frame of the scope.

165

Dolly In / Dolly Out

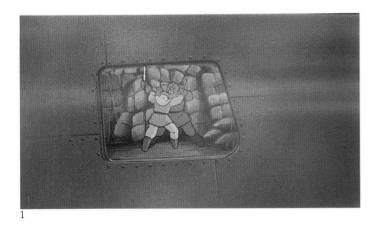

1

(1)–(4) A method generally known as rotation dolly out makes the hold of the Brig rotate and depicts it from the viewpoint of a rapidly receding Nausicaä.

(5)–(7) The camera is simply always dolly in on Yupa, but sliding of the background between the foreground animation and the book cel (trees of the Sea of Decay) is added, producing the sense that the camera (Nausicaä on *Mehve*) is entering deeper into the frame. In this way, although this is dolly in, dolly out for a flat drawing, it's possible to depict various things by adding in multiple elements.

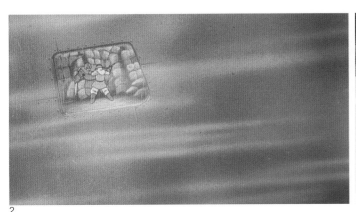

2

5

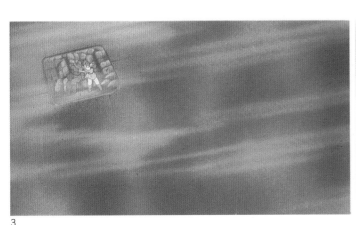

3

6

4

7

Background Animation

1

3

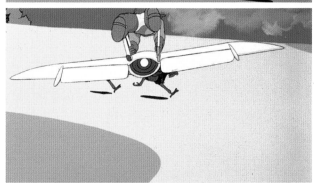

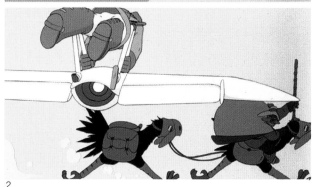

2

(1) Gunship dropping below the clouds.
(2) Nausicaä intercepting Yupa's party.
(3) Large Ohm herd exploding across the desert.
Given that the background in cel animation is flat, it's not possible for the camera to follow (or retreat from) a character as they go deeper in, so background animation is used instead.

Image Processing

In animation, main image processing is roughly split up into cel processing and film processing. Like the camerawork discussed earlier, these two techniques are much more often use in combination than alone, and close coordination is required between all production departments to determine the final look of the image.

Coloring

Simply painting the cels according to the color direction is one way to depict the texture and status of objects. This can be an extremely effective method of showing changes in color due to transparency or the location of the light source, as in the examples given here. It's the very close collaboration between color design and background art that allows us to achieve these kinds of results. In particular, the water shots in (1) and (2), and the inside and outside of the light in (3) could not succeed without this collaboration.

1

2

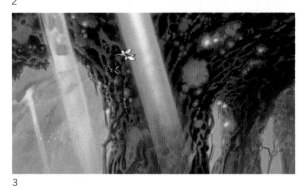

3

4

(1) No water was drawn in the background. The only depiction of water is the coloring around the beaks of the horseclaws.
(2) Having the inner part of the water painted on the cels and then moved brings out a sense of transparency and flow.
(3) Insects moving through the light.
(4) This shot is a wonderful depiction that comes from coloring only the movement of the light source.

Color Carbon

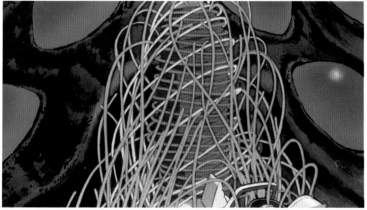

This method allows you to change the color of a character silhouette to any color other than the conventional carbon black when you copy the animation lines to a cel with a fax machine. It's effective in depicting something that would lose its texture with black solid lines. The idea is similar to color tracing.

In the film, this was used for the Ohm tentacles and the Giant Warriors (parts). You can use colors such as red, blue, yellow, brown, and white.

Touch

This is a method of applying paint with a brush so that faint traces of it show on the front of a standard colored cel. As in the example stills here, it's used to express "dirt" on a character, among other things. In particular, it produces an almost tragic effect on Nausicaä's injured body.

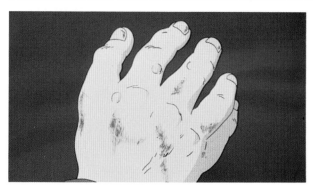

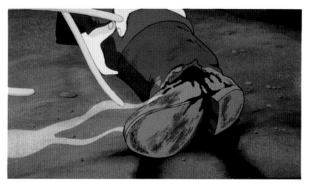

Double Exposure

1

2

3

(1) Ohm eye. However, Nausicaä alone is not double exposure. Her coloring was changed according to specific color direction, so the background is the only part the color of the transparent Ohm eye actually interferes with through double exposure.

(2) Ohm blood dyeing Nausicaä's clothing.

(3) Nausicaä through the shell colored with different color direction (top). The shadow through the shell is double exposure (bottom).

(4) Amniotic fluid of the artificial womb holding the Giant Warrior.

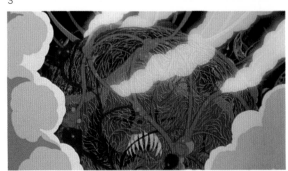

4

Superimposition

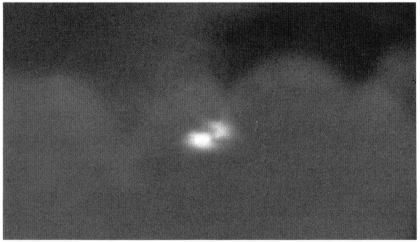 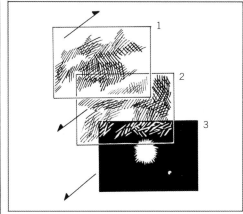

The strange white light (transport ship) moving in the cloudy night sky was done by sliding a superimposed character above the background. In this case, the light-emitting character (3) was superimposed through two sliding masks (1, 2). The two masks were given cloudy patches of light and shade with brushes, and the shape of the light source is always changing.

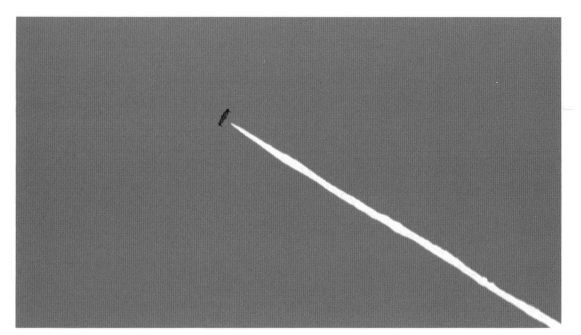

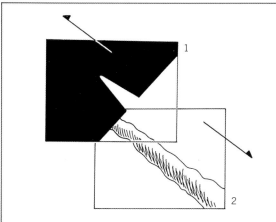

The gunship's (Asbel's) vapor trail is also superimposition. The vapor trail is drawn entirely in advance, matching the trajectory of the gunship (2). The movement created by superimposing the vapor trail while sliding a mask at the same speed as the gunship (1) set on the background.

Overlap (Fade-in, Fade-out)

2

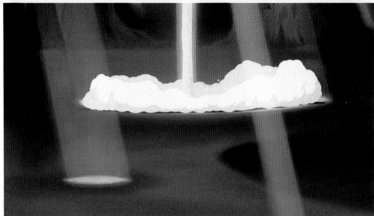

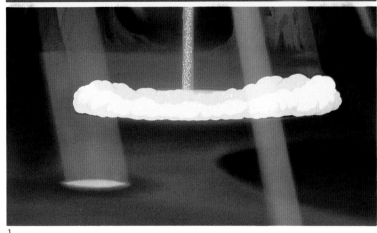

1

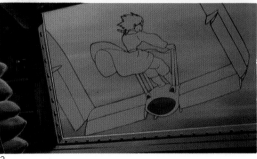

(1) In order to maintain the sense of weight of the sand pouring down from the ceiling, we made two streams of sand and then overlapped both.

(2) Ohm eyes changing color. Two cels were made for the eyes alone and overlapped. This is a fairly basic use of overlap.

(3) The cel is replaced with overlap to try and produce a sense of melting into the clouds, a feeling of space. In this shot, the overlap is applied when Nausicaä is on the verge of leaving the Brig storeroom and slipped beneath the cloud (airbrush) cel.

3

1

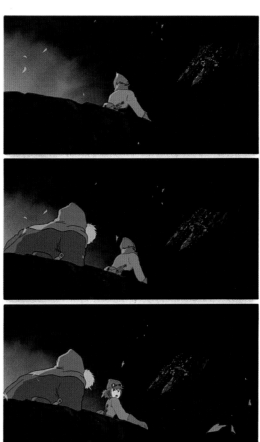

2

(1) At first glance, it looks as though the camera is receding from the image as they disappear in the light, but the people on horses in this cut are faded out while tracking back. This produces a strange effect because the animation is done not by reduction but with mechanical filming.

(2) For the surface of the mountain that pops up and disappears with the movement of the large ship, we made three cels for just the parts where the light shone separately from the background mountains (book cel), matched this with the source of the light (the ship), and switched them out while connecting by fading in and out.

Wipe

Conventionally, this method is used to change frames; a separate image appears from part of the frame (unspecified), and this spreads out, erasing the previous image to change the whole frame into something new. Here, this "wipe" is used in an animation sense; the rippling change of the Ohms' blue eyes is actually not animation, but rather a separate image synthesized through filming.

Transparent Light Graffiti
From Sirius to proton beam

1

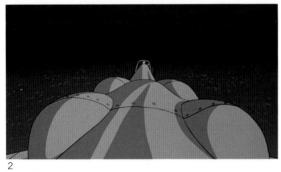

2

5

3

6

4

(1) Light spreading out from the tips of the tentacles. The surrounding light is airbrush and is made gradually stronger with overlap.

(2) Sirius glittering ahead of the gunship. We were aiming to depict a natural star, rather than a cross shape.

(3) An eerie red light behind Nausicaä (Ohm).

(4) The light of the gunship thrusters. Skilled coloring direction for the background and the cel combine to produce a wonderful atmosphere.

(5) Light from the grains of sand at the bottom of the Sea of Decay reflecting the sunlight pouring in.

(6) Electrical emission inside the clouds (lightning). This effect was produced not just with the power of transmitted light, but also color design that enhanced the contrasts.

7

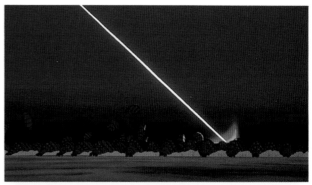

9

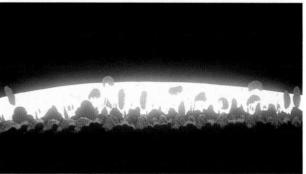

10

(7), (8) The proton beam and the nuclear explosion it causes. Transmitted light itself has a power that coloring just can't compare with. Here, the power of animation and the transmitted light unify, producing a shot with serious impact.

(9) Tank guns. The light on the other side of the scrapped ship is airbrush.

(10) The flare launched by the gunship.

Both (9) and (10) are shots filled with reality thanks to the movement and the simple shape of the light source, in marked contrast with (7) and (8).

8

Filter

Rippled glass

This is used in places to create distortion, mainly used when depicting the air as being unstable, such as with flames. The stills are representative of this, the scene of a fire.

D Filter

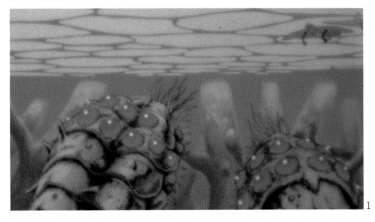

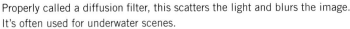

1

2

3

Properly called a diffusion filter, this scatters the light and blurs the image.
It's often used for underwater scenes.
(1) Typical example of use underwater.
(2) Also produces results in a reminiscing scene.
(3) A room saturated with steam.

P.L. Filter (Polarization)

One type of polarizing filter was used in all aspects of this film because it prevents the greatest enemy of filming: cel damage. The cels used in animation are very easy to damage, and depending on the conditions, this damage might show up in the actual animation, ruining all the work put into it. Because of this, damaged cels must be retaken at the stage before filming, posing a serious risk to the production budget and the schedule, among other things. This filter handily solves this problem. But a side effect of this filter is that it affects the color of the image. This is particular noticeable with white and black, causing the former to leap out and the latter to sink back. If this sort of filter gains broader use, this impact will have to be considered from the color design stage (concept art, color direction).

The Road to *Nausicaä*

Animage Editorial Division

The idea was that I would write in detail about the sequence of events from the Animage editorial division's first contact with Hayao Miyazaki to the serialization of the manga *Nausicaä of the Valley of the Wind* and the manga's subsequent transformation into a movie, including detailed film production notes, but I ran into a wall right out of the gate.

I was hoping to get everyone to submit their notes and things from the time and build the story from there, but of course, not a single one of us was organized enough to actually have anything like that neatly set aside. So while everyone was still digging around in their desks, muttering, "They have to be in here somewhere," we ran out of time. Thus, I'd like to start by discussing something relatively fresh in our memories—how *Nausicaä* became a film.

The series gains momentum

I'm pretty sure it was in November 1982. It had been almost a year already since *Nausicaä* started running in the *Animage*. Several other magazines and newspapers had given the series good reviews, and it was consistently in the top five in our own reader survey; the work was getting a lot of attention.

The first review appeared in the May 1982 issue of *Variety* (Kadokawa Shoten) and featured manga artist Katsuhiro Otomo openly praising the work:

The excellence of Miyazaki's art isn't simply in the expressiveness of the faces of his characters, or in his ability to capture a scene in a sketch; he understands how to show off an image. Why on earth is it that this essential pleasure of manga—something manga seems to have lost lately—comes through in the work of people who have worked in anime? The props are fascinating. He devotes attention to each of the kites, each rifle that appears in his pages. You get the sense that Miyazaki is laser-focused on his own tastes and ideas, that he's really having a good time drawing this series. It's hard to put into words, but despite the fact that we've seen only two chapters so far, you understand only too well that this is poetry. There are beautiful scenes. You sometimes forget that it's a manga.

Additionally, when posed the question "What was the most interesting manga of 1982?" (*Petit Flower*, Shogakukan, December 1982), Keiko Takemiya responded, "Nausicaä." She expanded upon why:

I've been reading since the first episode, and as someone also in the industry, my gut feeling was excitement, that this was the beginning of a whole new world. A manga artist's

mission is to invite the reader into a totally different world. And in that sense, I think this is a truly marvelous work.

And there were many other reviews, appearing in places like *Monthly OUT, Yomiuri Shimbun*, and Tokyo Shimbun. The manga industry magazine *Comic Box* (November/December 1982) even put together a 70-page special on Miyazaki and *Nausicaä*.

Ten-minute pilot proposal

Animage editor-in-chief Hideo Ogata was very sensitive to the fact that the manga was being noticed. "Maybe we should make a pilot film? About five minutes long?" he suggested to the editorial division.

He had no idea how we'd make something like that or where we'd show it, nothing. I suppose it was that Japanese stereotype where you start running before you know where you're going. And everyone else in the editorial division was similarly irresponsible. "That's a great idea," we said, even though we didn't know the first thing about it. Everything developed from this lone question.

And then a week or so went by before the next idea popped up: we could premiere it at 1982's Budokan's Anime Gran Prix, that May 23. "Let's do it. A pilot could lead to a movie."

Everyone was completely on board. The impatient Ogata immediately went out to Miyazaki's house in Saitama Prefecture, dragging the Nausicaä editor along with him.

"Five minutes? I won't be able to depict anything," Miyazaki replied immediately, upon hearing the proposal.

"Even just a peek into Nausicaä's world would be good."

"Still, I'd have to draw something at any rate for just that glimpse…"

They went back and forth for a few minutes until Ogata blurted, "How about ten minutes then?"

And just like that, the time had doubled. Miyazaki considered this for a while.

"Well, if it's ten minutes," he said.

The details of the video they discussed were quite similar to the proposal that came later, and this was where they left things for the day. But by the time Ogata and the editor left Miyazaki's house, they looked smugly satisfied, as though the ten-minute version of Nausicaä was a done deal. They were happy people.

But it turned out that although Miyazaki might have been willing and able to make a ten-minute film, finishing it for May 23 was completely beyond the realm of the possible. The editor continued to discuss the particulars with Miyazaki, and we came to understand a number of things.

First of all, it would cost a fair bit of money. Even if Miyazaki directed, wrote the storyboards, and did the art himself, we would still have to hire an art director. We'd also need an animator. And you have to have a production assistant. Plus, we'd have to find people for the cinematography and the dubbing. When we thought about it, ten minutes was nearly half of an episode of a TV show; it was only natural that it would be hard. We calculated the production costs and discovered the whole endeavor would easily cost more than five million yen.

And whatever else was going on, we had a magazine to put out, so the editorial division couldn't exactly go around asking people to do the final processing or anything. A production assistant at a certain animation studio heard about our little project and warned us we'd be better off walking away from the whole thing. "There are so many TV shows right now, even we're having trouble finding animators and other people, and we're a known face in the industry."

70-minute special proposal

We were also very busy, which helped, and the pilot film proposal started to fade away. It was at the end of November that it reemerged.

Within the Tokuma Shoten Group, there was a company called Tokuma Communications and their purpose was the sale of videos. So they had the idea of turning our ten-minute short into a thirty-minute video. It hadn't even been a month since we were talking about five minutes and we were already somehow at thirty.

Miyazaki and Ogata discussed the idea.

"Thirty minutes is sort of neither here nor there. If we had an hour and ten minutes—the length of a TV special—we could make a little something that really speaks…"

In the blink of an eye, we were up to an hour and ten minutes.

According to Miyazaki, the video would be something along the lines of Nausicaä's childhood. Heir to the Valley of the Wind, Nausicaä started training with a kite to become a grown wind rider when she was five. A "wind rider" was someone who had learned how to read the flow of the air through training and could thus detect the danger of spores from the Sea of Decay and help people and animals attacked by Ohm. The video would show a young Nausicaä growing up through her meetings with scholar and sword master Yupa, and with the small Ohm. That was the gist of it.

This was extremely interesting and promised to turn into something very good. If we could sell it as a video, we had no doubt it would be revolutionary in the video world.

Once again, we calculated the production costs. It was an absurdly massive sum, totally out of line with projected profits. In the case of an average video, The Castle of Cagliostro, the film was already done. So Tokuma Communications could use that for 19,800 yen. But given that our film would cost however many hundreds of thousands of yen (very near a billion), it would have been difficult to recover that. We were

making these calculations for the number of pages and the density of Miyazaki's work, however. If it had been a normal TV movie, it probably wouldn't have cost so much.

"If we're going to do it, make a movie!" The idea came from no one in particular.

"Right. Let's do it."

This project was a truck that was already out of control. We didn't know where it was going to stop. All this was sometime in late December.

Ogata ran around in the company trying to drum up excitement. Several incredible, miraculous stars came into alignment, and suddenly, we were making a movie. But before I get to that, I'd like to touch on the sequence of events from the time the Animage editorial division first spoke with Miyazaki up until the serialization of the manga Nausicaä.

Three months of meeting anime reporters

Flipping through Animage, it seems we first met Miyazaki when he made Future Boy Conan for Nippon Animation. The article detailed a Nippon Animation studio visit, so Conan wasn't necessarily the focus of the piece. Similarly, the interview wasn't with the Miyazaki, a fact that would come to be loaded with all kinds of meaning in later years, but rather with a slightly unapproachable middle-aged man wearing a sun visor. But, well, this was when the the bit was being created, so there's really no helping that.

"We got another toy again today." This was from the man sitting beside him—seen from the present, the Yasuo Otsuka.

"We're not making the sort of work that could sell that." And this was again a strange man in a hunting cap. The anime magazine had only launched three months earlier, so we knew even less than the fans.

The next time Miyazaki showed up in Animage was with The Castle of Cagliostro. The article was in the November 1979 issue, so the interview would have been conducted at the end of August or in September.

"And they wouldn't really let us get a shot of their faces." The editor in charge of the piece grumbles about this even now.

Otsuka was sitting beside Miyazaki this time as well. He started playing with a kendama spike and ball for some reason, and Miyazaki suddenly looked back and said he'd sit for a picture as long as they were playing kendama. A picture of the pair playing kendama was printed in Animage.

We couldn't get a new kendama picture for the next issue, so we had no choice but to reuse the one from the previous issue. "For some reason, Miyazaki is playing kendama again this month," we noted beneath the photo.

Miyazaki was angry. "Please behave yourselves."

I think it was the interview for that issue when we tried to get closer to Miyazaki for a comment, and Otsuka stopped us.

"Oh! Don't, you can't. It's not safe, so please stay back."

Apparently, Miyazaki did not bother with comments and the like once he was immersed in production. Even so, we did manage to get a couple words from him.

The Castle of Cagliostro was released in December 1979. At the beginning of the following year, Miyazaki's only public work was episode 145 and the finale of Shin Lupin. He appeared in the magazine twice: in June 1980's "Hayao Miyazaki's Check and Point" and October's "Lupin Requiem."

Although it wasn't exactly a smash hit in theaters, appreciation of *Castle of Cagliostro* began to surge among fans. In December 1980, the film was shown on television, so we pushed and got Miyazaki to appear in a conversation with *Animage*, his first conversation in an anime magazine.

Film plan encounter

Between 1979 to 1981, we had put together specials for *Animage*, but in the spring of 1981, Miyazaki was popular enough that we could objectively sell copies with "The World of Hayao Miyazaki." This was realized in the August 1981 issue with "Manga Movie Magician Hayao Miyazaki: A World of Adventure and Romance."

This essay has thus far been a bit long-winded, but I've written of time of our first meeting with Miyazaki so that you might get a sense of how this special issue would have never come about with those two and a half years. And without this "World of Hayao Miyazaki," we would never have published *Nausicaä*.

At thirty-two pages, it was a rather long special, but thanks to a piece by Isao Takahata in his refined style, we managed to succeed content-wise. More importantly, this special had a knock-on effect. Among the sea of illustrations Miyazaki had drawn were plans for any number of films.

"I want to make this sort of film, you see?" He passionately detailed one concept after another for us, and Ogata's editorial division began to wonder if there wasn't something we could be doing to make one of them happen.

Succinctly put, it was simple. But it seems the habit of running before you've really thought anything through is a hard one to break.

At the beginning of July, we submitted the Animage anime film proposal at a "movie meeting" with affiliated companies such as Tokuma Shoten, Daiei, and Tokuma Music—currently Tokuma Japan. And of course, Miyazaki would be directing this film. He even drew several illustrations for us to present. He was quick to draw this kind of thing for us. Titled Sengoku Majo (we at Animage just went ahead and gave it this title), it was the story of a boy born into a world of warring states as he bravely faces an intruder who suddenly appears from another world.

"In this era, you have large statues of Buddha lying on their sides in the grass," Miyazaki noted. "This is what I want to draw, the powerful forms of the famed Bando warriors in a wasteland."

Naturally, Miyazaki's unique machines would make an appearance in this work as well. Not to mention an enormous demon castle floating in the sky. It sounded interesting. But after some reflection and discussion at the movie meeting, the project was postponed as being a bit premature.

"I'm used to not getting my hopes up," Miyazaki said,

but we at Animage couldn't accept it. We soon submitted a second proposal, Richard Corben's *Rowlf*, one of the many underground comics Tokyo Movie Shinsha president Yutaka Fujioka brought back from the United States. Miyazaki really loved it.

In the illustrations for the Rowlf plan, you can see what looks like the Valley of the Wind, Nausicaä, the Queen of the Ghouls, and Sand Ohms, among other things. These were not in the original Rowlf; the film plan didn't stop at Corben's original work. Incidentally, the extremely science-fictional setting of the Sea of Decay was also added to Rowlf, changing the form once more, transforming this film plan into the manga *Nausicaä of the Valley of the Wind*.

But it was another "no."

They say that for every TV anime on the air, sixty ideas were rejected, but that number is surely much larger in the case of film. We understood that most of our ideas would be thrown out. We were painfully aware that the whole endeavor would be near impossible without some kind of hook, like the original manga sold like gangbusters or Kurosawa was attached to direct. Or the story was ho-hum, but a famous singer was set to star. Something along those lines.

"Well, if there's no original manga, then we just have to make one, right?" Yutaka Wada said, casually. He was the director of marketing for Tokuma Shoten, and he followed through on the Animage film proposal later, our own personal cheerleader.

The phone call to stop before we even started

Under Ogata, the Animage Piranha Brigade immediately got to work. If Miyazaki ran a manga with us, sales would probably increase, and we might be able to turn it into a movie—the perfect plan, two birds with one stone.

This was no simple thing, but with the help and advice of Yasuo Otsuka, a consensus was reached that the manga would start in the January 1982 issue (on sale December 10).

Miyazaki had conditions, however:

① If he started work on an animation collaboration, the series would go on hiatus.

② He would draw what he wanted, though Editorial could cancel the series if it wasn't popular.

③ He wouldn't draw it with an anime as the end goal. More specifically, he wouldn't adopt a style guaranteed to go over with general audiences. As much as possible, he wanted to use new and innovative panel arrangements and art styles. The manga might actually end up being difficult to turn into an anime.

He picked up his pen and started to draw in September, but given that the concept took time to sort out, combined with the fact that it had been a decade or so since he had drawn manga, his progress was quite slow. Eventually, the series was postponed a month and scheduled to start in the February issue.

I think it was around the end of October that he told us the title: *Nausicaä of the Valley of the Wind*. We thought it was a good title, cool and clear.

The first episode was partially completed by the middle of December. It showed an Ohm coming out of the Sea of Decay. Although it was shocking in its power, we felt strangely uncertain about it. The art style was something we were completely unfamiliar with. Later readers in the editorial division and the general public felt the same uncertainty. The audience was probably divided evenly.

Unlike today's manga, which lends itself to a quick trip diagonally through the panels, each and every panel tripped us up, forcing us to read much more carefully. There was so much information in each panel that the manga was difficult to read in a certain sense. But this strange world was Miyazaki's aim right from the start.

Funnily, a few pages in that first episode are in a style that's fashionable now—or rather entirely normal. The characters really move in this style, but you don't really feel like you're transported to another world these days.

In any case, the first episode was finished by December 20, the work of submitting over, so we were heaving a collective sigh of relief when we got a terrible phone call. From Miyazaki, of course.

"I want to stop the publication."

Stop it? The issue with the first episode hadn't even gone on sale yet. We were all utterly baffled. His editor alone understood what was going on.

Ogata was puzzled. "I wonder why he wants to stop?"

This understanding editor endeavored to explain as they rushed over to Telecom in Koenji in Tokyo, where Miyazaki worked at the time.

In the summer of 1981, Miyazaki was working with Yoshifumi Kondo, Kazuhide Tomonaga, and Tsukasa Tannai on the designs for *Sherlock Hound*. People would come from Italy for meetings, and although it looked like things would be ready to go at any moment, it still took three weeks for letters to arrive (the Italian mail service was slow), and the collaborative project wasn't really making much progress, given the differences in thinking when it came to the characters. The Italians were fussy about all sorts of things, like no guns pointed at people, no bloodshed, no theft of religious objects, etc.

So Miyazaki didn't know when production for this project would actually start, which is why he was interested in doing a manga series. The Animage editorial division basically lucked into this opening in his schedule.

I think it was at the start of November 1982 that production on *Hound* finally started. (I guess they'd basically come to an agreement with the Italian side.) Still, the whole project was scheduled to take several times longer than your average TV program. Miyazaki's editor was relieved, and Miyazaki himself thought it could all work out somehow.

But he pours everything he has into every project he works on. The first episode of the manga series was incredible, and he didn't hold back with *Hound* either. He used every extra second of the inflated schedule to improve the quality of the work. (He was looking at 10,000 cels with essentially no repetition.)

All of which meant that Miyazaki was averaging three hours of sleep a night in December. No matter how late he'd been up the previous night, he would leave for the office at ten in the morning, come home at eleven at night, and then draw manga until five or so in the morning. This grueling schedule would put anyone at their wits' end.

Unprecedented pencil drawings

"So that's the long and short of it."

Now that Miyazaki's reasoning had been explained to him, Ogata naturally became serious. He understood the situation, but still, to simply stop the series…

"We'll ask him anyway," he replied. And so he, deputy editor Suzuki, and Miyazaki's editor marched into Telecom together.

Yasuo Otsuka was also in attendance. He encouraged the editorial division side, saying "You can't stop now," but after an hour of fierce debate, Miyazaki's resolve was unchanged. Perhaps it really was the end. Just as we were about to give up, Miyazaki spoke, offering an opening for a new direction.

"If I could do it in pencil, I can draw a lot faster…"

We snapped at this. "Pencil is absolutely fine."

"Really?" Miyazaki looked like he had seen the light of hope as well.

We decided he would do a test drawing in pencil and then we'd see how it printed up, and the matter was settled.

The test drawing worked well, and so the manga was drawn in pencil from the second episode on. (He did go back to drawing in pen after a little while. Please try and see if you can determine which pages are which in the edition currently on sale.)

And then a certain manga artist asked us: If *Nausicaä* is done in pencil, what does Miyazaki do for his first draft? It's true that if he did his rough sketches in pencil, then they would be printed along with the finished lines. (After all, it's not as though he could erase them.) Do please take a look at the original art if you get the chance, and if you do, you'll see that he used a light-blue pencil for the first draft. He also used blue to note where the screen tone should go. He did the rough composition in blue pencil and then finished it up in pencil. For more complicated sections, he drew in pencil on a separate piece of paper and then put that paper underneath the manga page and traced it, a practice made possible by the custom animation desk at which he worked.

In this way, he finished sixteen pages for both the March and April 1982 issues, but this fell to ten pages for the May issue, twelve in June, and twelve in July. And as the number of pages dropped, the number of complaining letters from readers went up. They wanted to read more. And we wanted to print more. But even though he was moving faster in pencil, this was still almost more than he could manage because this time around March, April, and May corresponded precisely with the peak of *Hound* production. Once that hump was passed, he drew twenty-four pages in one burst for our August issue. He had the extra time since *Hound* production was in a deadlock of sorts, with issues on the Italian side.

Eventually, the combined efforts of Miyazaki and the animation and art staff at Telecom had produced four episodes, and then the project was essentially shelved. Wondering if there wasn't some way to have them broadcast in Japan, Animage put together specials in the September 1982 issue, and then in February, March, and May of 1983. In the March issue, Fujiko Fujio commented, "I was allowed to see two episodes. Every single one of the animation backgrounds was wonderful, the kind of lovely work you rarely see." Shinichi Suzuki also spoke highly of it, "You could spend all day heaping praise on the show, and it still wouldn't be enough."

Cure for drowsiness

Miyazaki did the screen tone himself for the first episode of the series, but he asked manga artist Takeshi Tetsuro to do it from the second episode on. This was another way to save time. His editor could have done it perhaps, but it was a rather time-consuming endeavor. Consider this as you flip through those pages. Someone had to cut out each and every one of those Ohm legs, far beyond the ability of a short-tempered editor.

So Takeshi and the editor would settle into the workroom on the second floor of Miyazaki's house and wait for the art to be finished as they poured tea and watched over him. Miyazaki would talk about all kinds of things as he drew. If he got too into his story, he would whirl around and begin to talk in earnest, so they made sure to cut him off in the right places. It seems like a small thing, but Animage is all about the details.

In the middle of the night, his wife would bring onigiri rice balls and miso soup for us. This feast was absurdly delicious, but the problem was, we would get sleepy. So then Miyazaki's stories would become about getting our blood moving and beating back the drowsiness. Most of these tales were about airplanes. The story of 1920s aviator Jean Mermoz was particularly exciting.

Flying over the Andes in an unreliable aircraft, Mermoz had to make an emergency landing on the mountainside. Miraculously, he survived, but his plane was in pieces and the temperature was -15°C. With nothing to eat, he endured the cold for four whole days, repaired the plane, and then pushed the 2,500-kilogram vehicle up to the top of the slope, slid down the steep rock-strewn incline toward the valley, and miraculously returned alive. A true story that sounds like it couldn't possibly be.

Wind, Sand and Stars by another aviator, Saint-Exupéry, was also a favorite of Miyazaki's. It contains the line, "The Earth teaches us more about ourselves than all the books in the world, because it is resistant to us."

The instinctual desire to restore the natural world and the physical pleasure of flight can always be seen in Miyazaki's work, and there does seem to be some commonality in the stories of Mermoz and *Wind, Sand, and Stars*. This appears most directly in *Nausicaä of the Valley of the Wind*.

Wind, Sand, and Stars also features the line "No one ever returns from winter in the Andes." It would be interesting to turn a story of an adventurer that begins with this into an anime—or rather, Miyazaki wanted to make it; he seemed very interested in it.

"But what would spur them (the aviators) to such lengths..." He would always start spinning his story. But they still had a deadline.

"Hmm, how many pages left again?" They would carefully bring him back to reality every so often.

The series went smoothly after that, but Miyazaki did take a break once for the November 1982 issue because he went to the United States for another joint project, separate from *Hound*. And then he quit Telecom at the end of October. He had a number of reasons for leaving, no doubt, but the editorial division was just delighted that we could ask for more pages now. His editor was overjoyed that getting those pages would no longer be like pulling teeth...although this turned out to be wrong. We were selfish.

We got swept up in the confusion of this time and decided to do a bonus manga for the *Animage* paperback: *The Journey of Shuna*. In the beginning, however, he apparently had other ideas in mind, stories like a plane that didn't fly, built in secret by a certain European country during World War II. If the opportunity arises, we'd love to have him write these bonus stories, too.

The series had been going for a year, the reviews were good, it was being picked by all kinds of newspapers and magazines. Here, we finally come full circle to Ogata running around, trying to turn the manga into a movie after the five-minute pilot proposal.

(And I breathe a sigh of relief. But this was such a jump back in time, it must be difficult to actually follow. Given Takahata and Miyazaki never jumped back in time without deep and serious thought, they would no doubt get mad at me if they read this.)

In-house consensus

December 1982. *Animage* editorial division's desire to make the film became conviction. But how would we actually make it happen? We lacked a realistic plan, as well as know-how and experience, so we were simply moving intently, instinctively.

First of all, it was clear we needed a consensus within the company. There were plenty of people more important than Ogata. At the top of this VIP mountain was, of course, the president. And an "audience" for Miyazaki with this president came to be on December 21. Perhaps some fans are scratching their heads at this. Yes, the 21st was the day of the Animage Ase Mamire release party. This was the day that Miyazaki spoke on behalf of Takahata and Otsuka, who were both in the United States.

Miyazaki, the president, Ogata, and Miyazaki's editor ate shabu-shabu and drank. The conversation moved from topic to topic, from Chinese animation to politics.

"Drink hard and go hard, and the lecture will go well," the president said, as he refilled glasses.

Miyazaki seemed a little drunk. But his 2:00 lecture went well. He talked about a certain woman from the processing inspection, and it was the end of the year, everyone rushing about, so this was a good story, one that warmed the heart while also sobering the mind.

His concluding lines were also solid: "There are three conditions necessary to achieve something. These are things that everyone here in this venue has. Be young, be poor, and be unknown. Fight for your grand ambitions."

Without any concrete progress on the movie in 1982, we turned the calendar page to 1983. The film would come to life in the span of mere months from now, incredibly. It was like a divine hand was at work, nudging us forward. Perhaps this was actually proof of how powerful the manga truly was.

In January, a certain film industry insider very much wanted "to make *Nausicaä* our next anime film, although this is still just a desire at the moment." Nonetheless, we were very happy to hear it.

"First of all, the setting is great. It fits perfectly with the 'futuristic sense' of young people lately. Also, I'm confident that the single beam of light as the existence of hope will also be appealing."

"The machines are good, too. Those curving lines give them a real warmth. Young people are used to seeing cold machines with hard lines, so this should be exciting and fresh!"

"There's a trend in the world of anime films toward director so-and-so's works. Given the sheer power Miyazaki showed us with *Conan* and *The Castle of Cagliostro*, you could even say it's strange no one's putting out his own work."

Nothing could have given us more hope than these comments.

In February, we started talking about how we wanted to put out an image album at Animage Level (Tokuma Japan). This ended up being "Tori no Hito (Bird person)" released on November 25, 1983. This wasn't directly connected with the making of the film, but it was proof we were building the right environment.

Sudden film adaptation development

I think it was the middle of February 1983. Wada, head of marketing at Tokuma Shoten, came to the editorial division and told us about a surprising occurrence that day. Because of his work, Wada was always talking with advertising agencies, and he had known the division responsible for Tokuma Shoten at Hakuhodo, the second largest ad agency in Japan, for some time.

What had surprised him on this particular day was the discovery that the Shiro Miyazaki in this sales division there was in fact the younger brother of Hayao Miyazaki. The youngest of four brothers, Shiro is a little bit of a better man than his older brother. This was nothing but fortuitous. The younger Miyazaki immediately started beating the drum and blowing the horn to everyone, including the head of the sales division, of course, for Hakuhodo to join the film production group. If they did, it was sure to be made.

The reaction came right away. This ad agency was, after all, on the leading edge of the era. The speed of this development stunned us. By the middle of February, it had basically been settled that the publisher and the ad agency would put forth their own separate capabilities, and make the film a joint production.

The film would obviously be great for Tokuma Shoten, but Hakuhodo also stood to benefit from the work. As one step in the M/E (marketing/engineering; the agency was quick to let the abbreviations fly, bewildering our deputy editor and his poor English), Nausicaä was perfect for the first shot fired on behalf of a future long-term project. Even we, with our poor understanding of the alphabet soup, could see that the film adaptation was finally becoming a reality. We were overjoyed.

Once the general overview was decided, it was time for the itemized agenda. March and April saw incremental progress on the questions of distribution, production, time in theaters, budget, staff, content, publicity, and more, each of these overlapping in fine ways with the others.

With Ogata leading us, we were mainly involved with the budget, the staff, the content, and the publicity. Considering the fact that Animage was an anime magazine and we were publishing the original series—not to mention that we had daily contact with Miyazaki—it was only natural we would have to take the lead in these areas. We pushed back publicity for the time being to focus on budget, staff, and content.

We got Miyazaki's help putting together the budget. We came to understand that just as a piece of land has a declared value and a market price, the reality of this budget was hard to get a good grasp on. Who we hired to work on the film would also depend on the movie Miyazaki was planning to make. Despite the fact that we did have the original manga, it was obvious that the movie would necessarily be different from the epic unfinished manga.

Put together a budget, negotiate with staff, discuss the story with Miyazaki—we discovered that this was far too much work for us to handle. That said, we absolutely couldn't push it all off onto Miyazaki. He already had a massive amount of work to do, with directing, writing the script, doing the storyboards, designing the backgrounds and setting, and more.

Things kept marching forward, however, as we wrestled with all of this. It was April when we decided on Toei for distribution. In the discussions with Toei, it became clear that it would be best if the film hit theaters in March of the following year.

In April, Miyazaki had his back up against the wall with *The Journey of Shuna* (it had already been delayed two months), and in the latter half of the month, he was writing Nausicaä; he only attended one of the film production committee meetings—although he was still in constant communication with the editorial division). We consulted with him about whether or not production could really be finished in time for a March theatrical release. Miyazaki pulled out some animation paper, which he always used for notes, and did the back calculation for the schedule several times.

Open in theaters in March, right... So recording and dubbing in February. Animation's done in January. In-betweens finished in December. So then...at the latest, we start animation work by August 1. Half of the storyboard at that time. Script at the end of June. Designs in May... That'll be rough!! It's already the middle of April.

No matter how many times he did the calculation, the fact that it would be rough going didn't change. And Miyazaki also had conditions: We had to decide on a production studio by the middle of May. And one more thing: Isao Takahata would be the producer.

"Takahata? You mean that Takahata?"

"Yes, I mean Paku. C'mon, it's a great idea, right?"

Yasuo Otsuka had been technically attached to everything Miyazaki had done up to that point (*Conan*, *The Castle of Cagliostro*) as animation director, but according to what we heard from various people involved, he had actually fulfilled something of a producer role. When Miyazaki started working on something, he poured all his efforts into raising the quality of that project, so he apparently needed someone to take the reins in a variety of senses. But Otsuka had an important position with *Little Nemo*. Meanwhile, Takahata had stepped down as director of that project and returned to Japan from the United States in March.

There's no need to go over again the relationship between and talents of these three men, who had produced any number of works that would go down in the history of anime at Toei Doga, A Productions, Zuiyo, Nippon Animation, and Telecom.

"I've spent far and away more time with them than with my wife and children," said Miyazaki.

I think that tells the story of their relationship quite well.

"We'll split the work…"

Two weeks after the initial request, Isao Takahata agreed to take on the role of producer. He said he decided to do it because, "I'm not just praying for him to succeed as a friend. I have this feeling that I want to split the work and share the joy of success again like we have in the past. I don't know if I'll actually be of any use, though…"

We went to the Takahata home so frequently that it became our war room until we got a formal one set up near Topcraft at the end of May. (Unlike a true war room, tea, cake, ice cream, and similar were laid out for us every half-hour. Miyazaki worried that he would get a pot belly.)

Miyazaki donned his helmet and made the trip from Saitama to Oizumi Gakuen on his motorcycle. He rode with such poise that he looked nothing like the wild riders of the time. In fact, a scooter would have suited him better.

At any rate, Miyazaki and Takahata had a million things to talk about. And not just talk, they needed to make decisions about each and every item: the studio, the staff. Neatly summed up in a single word, "staff" actually entailed reaching out to the animation director, the art director, a decent number of animators, someone for color design, and on and on, asking what their schedule was like and persuading them to get on board; naturally, this took time.

There was also plenty of work to do on the budget. Again, this wasn't simply a matter of adding up the unit costs for each part; they also had to incorporate all those subtle losses that someone who hadn't been in the trenches wouldn't know about, together with budget measures to secure the staff for everything, even though no staffing decisions had been made yet.

Of course, this kind of work was part of the making of any film, but given that he was a freelancer with no parent studio, we were actually unconsciously pushing the majority of the work onto Miyazaki himself. I can't deny that we got caught up in the idea that the movie was a done deal so long as we came up with the production capital.

"You're asking a lot of Miya by himself. Do you all actually realize that?" Takahata asked us, solemnly, when we were still discussing the role of producer with him. I remember it clear as day, and although he's never said so himself, I sometimes wonder if one big reason he agreed to be the producer was because of this. He couldn't just stand by and watch…

Around this time, Takahata also told us about a movie called *The Wages of Fear*. It was a tense, scary tale of a young driver and an older passenger driving a truck full of nitroglycerin into the depths of the jungle. The nitro would explode at the slightest jolt, so driver and passenger were understandably incredibly tense. As if unable to stand it any more, the driver snaps at the passenger, "Must be nice. You don't have to do anything."

And the older passenger replies, "Nicer to be driving. All I'm doing is sitting and being afraid."

The mental state of a producer was akin to that of this old man sitting fearful in the passenger seat, a deft comparison on the part of Yasuo Otsuka. Of course, given how Otsuka hated impertinence, this was likely self-effacing, but it was such a perfectly fitting turn of phrase that everyone burst out laughing.

The inventory of six or seven episodes of *Future Boy Conan* before the broadcast were used up in the blink of an eye, and the enormity of the last two months of *The Castle of Cagliostro* was still a topic of conversation. And now this film was also set to become a battlefield for a month or two… It was easy to guess at the mind-set of the producer on a Miyazaki film.

On May 4, Miyazaki finished *The Journey of Shuna* and traveled around for meetings for a few days. Most likely, he was trying to switch gears, to move beyond the manga he'd struggled with for months and re-energize himself. This trip was the turning point; when he locked himself up in his room to work after this, there was an obvious sharpness in his eyes and he was full of life. And no wonder. It was the first time he'd been on the frontlines in a while.

We continued to meet at Takahata's house, and in the middle of May, we officially decided on Topcraft for the production studio, and Miyazaki commuted to a nearby war room every day, until the real war room—a former yakiniku restaurant—was renovated. A former video arcade and bar, the room was covered in red with wall seating and carpets. Miyazaki brought a desk and chair and things in, and worked on the concept sketches here.

The arcade/bar had only just recently gone under, so every so often, strangers would wander in.

"Oh. Huh? Where's the owner? What happened?"

"The arcade closed two days ago."

"Hmm."

There were apparently a lot of these "customers" who would eventually go home without really getting the point, looking bewildered at the idea of someone drawing pictures in an arcade.

Tokyo Gas also stopped by. "We're here to check the meter. Oh, what are you doing?"

"Sketching. The arcade went out of business."

"Hmm. Well, that's a problem." Not looking much like it actually was a problem, the Tokyo Gas person glanced at Miyazaki's drawings, not really understanding what was going on. "See you tomorrow."

"I'm sure the owner of this place ran off in the middle of the night," Miyazaki noted, somewhat gleefully. He seemed to be enjoying himself.

That reminds me. When Fumihiko Takayama of Macross came to hang out at Topcraft, his old haunt, he spotted Miyazaki along the way and ended up following him. The director of MOSPEADA, Katsuhisa Yamada, was also still on the roll at Topcraft then, and he would come every day to chat with Miyazaki in the Red Room and peek at the drawings.

"I said I'm the chief director on a new show. I wonder if I'm really okay here," Miyazaki told us, concerned.

Two pages a day

Miyazaki drew two concept sketches a day for a total of thirty pages, which doesn't seem like a lot, but you don't need to go all the way back to the Miyazaki-designed demon castle in *Puss in Boots* to know that setting in his work is closely connected with the story. He creates stages that are ready for a play. The castle in *The Castle of Cagliostro* wasn't only an exterior; he created it taking into consideration who would be where doing what. He often said that the setting was no good unless the layout popped up in your mind once you were finished watching. Which I suppose is why he could only do two pages a day at best. And because he also had his original manga, done in his own hand, he probably didn't really need many more pages that this.

The first concept sketch he drew was, of course, *Nausicaä of the Valley of the Wind*. "She looks too quiet here," he muttered as he scribbled page after page. Or "Now she's just a showgirl." He scrapped plenty of potential looks.

While he was busy with the concept sketches, we urgently needed to get the staff together. But we stumbled upon all kinds of problems here after just a moment's thought.

The first was the schedule. We needed people who could finish everything between summer and the beginning of the following year. The second was that if they were attached to a production studio, it would be difficult for them to work on a one-off film. Moreover, Miyazaki wanted everyone to report to Topcraft every day for work. In other words, he wanted a structure that would allow frequent discussion, although this wasn't an absolute requirement. He did have one other requirement, however: that they be "good," of course.

So we needed talented freelancers with open schedules who could work in-house. If there was such an animator out there, no studio worth their salt would let them stay that way.

At any rate, we made a list and decided to reach out to the twenty or so people on it. It goes without saying that Takahata and Miyazaki were to be the center of the negotiations, but Ogata and the rest of us at the anime magazine knew much more about current young animators, having met or worked with any number of them. So we took the lead in reaching out to them. Takahata and Miyazaki had been at the same studios from Toei Doga to Telecom, so they basically knew the same

animators, a weak point that we were more or less able to make up for.

Fortunately, animation director Kazuo Komatsubara and art director Mitsuki Nakamura readily consented despite the condition that they be in-house, and the hiring of staff finally started to gain momentum.

We'd actually been in contact with Yoshinori Kanada, the standard-bearer for the third generation of anime, in the editorial division from the time we started to see concrete progress on the movie discussions in March.

Miyazaki also had high hopes for him. "Telecom's Kazuhide (Tomonaga) said he's really good."

Kanada apparently needed to steel himself to gain the resolve to join a Miyazaki project; he only formally came on board in May after talking for several hours with Miyazaki. We then had him meet with Takahata as well, which is when we first found out Kanada had worked on the video *Panda! Go, Panda!* Takahata was also surprised at the mysterious connection.

Kanada then recommended Osamu Nabeshima. Nabeshima had already agreed to work on another project, so it didn't look like it was going to pan out. But that other project was still up in the air in a number of ways, and our instincts told us we had a shot.

Miyazaki also strongly expressed his desire to have him on board. "In my experience, good people who are said to be good are definitely good. I'd love for you to join our team."

"Oh no, someone like me…" Nabeshima said in a voice that threatened to disappear, but he did later accept, as you well know.

Takashi Nakamura was also someone we'd had our eye on. Fortunately, we had a video tape of Nakamura's Gold Lightan, so we had Miyazaki watch it.

"There's a naturalness in the way he uses space and pauses," was his assessment.

Nakamura also said he wanted to work on a Miyazaki project. It took about two months from the time we first started talking with him, but he managed to rearrange his schedule and join our animation team.

Miyazaki was still doing the concept sketches when he started in on the synopsis, and at the end of May, he finished the first draft of the *Nausicaä* film plan, a moment to be celebrated. This first draft was written on five pages of large kent paper, and it goes without saying that it went through several revisions before becoming the basis for the storyboards.

For instance, the first page had something roughly like the below written on it:

—Prologue: Simple setup of era
• Yupa visits a city swallowed up by the Sea of Decay.
(Dead Ohm, city attacked by insects)
Yupa saves a fox-squirrel (Teto) and kills an insect. Yupa is attacked. Insects close in on him.
• Opening credits
(Yupa running)
Various aspects of the Sea of Decay, ruins of fallen civilization
• From the Sea of Decay to the desert. The whole of the

Ohm is revealed. Nausicaä. She soothes the Ohm and saves Yupa. Reunion of teacher and student. To the Valley of the Wind.

To Teto, Nausicaä. The girl's mysterious affinity.

• The miracle of green. The warm rusticness of the people of the Valley of the Wind. Wind rider. Nausicaä working. Castle. Jihl and Yupa. Nausicaä being adored by people.

• Dark night. Strong wind. People of the Valley sense something strange. Flashes of light racing through the Sea of Decay. Assaulted by insects, the ship from the city of Pejite (Brig) crashes in the valley. Lastelle hands the stone (energy fuel) to Nausicaä and dies. She learns of the occupation of the autonomous nation Pejite. Nausicaä sees the insects on the ship back to the Sea of Decay. Meets that Ohm. Nausicaä drawn to the Ohm.

From the end of May until the middle of June, Miyazaki and Takahata, along with Kazunori Ito, who had also been asked to work on the script, stared hard at those five pages of kent paper pinned to a wall in the Red Room. (We also tentatively offered our opinions.)

From the sidelines, we watched with utter astonishment the enormous energy and talent of these two men, Takahata stepping into the arena of a Miyazaki project and doing whatever he could to make it a success, Miyazaki climbing to ever greater heights as long as he was given the time to do so.

The conversation in the room veered from film theory to Shakespearean tragedy, and it would be utterly impossible to reproduce them here. Please allow me to simply touch on them briefly.

Too much story

• Deep in the Sea of Decay, the earth is being cleansed, but the issue is that this is not on the same time scale as Nausicaä's current human society (one in units of thousands of years, the other in decades). Doesn't this suggest that the future of humanity is, in the end, limited...?

• When we bring in the power struggle in the homeland of the Tolmekian, Kushana, occupying the Valley of the Wind, there's the risk of the story becoming overly bloated.

• "When the film ends, you must understand that Nausicaä is a human being caught between human society and the natural world."

"Nausicaä appears as a mysterious girl. In this film, that mysteriousness stops being mysterious."

"The interaction with the insects will probably be important."

"Why does Nausicaä love the Ohm even though the Ohm are supposedly loathed at this time? We have to make the audience see this objectively."

"We see the Ohm through Nausicaä's eyes in order to rouse empathy. She meets them, sees them, feels...I think we can get the audience to understand her love for them this way."

• "I'm concerned about time jumps. Is this the kind of movie where we can casually jump back and forth through time or not? Either is fine, but I want to choose one."

"Actually, I think time and space should flow linearly. I mean, *Star Wars* is all over the place."

"Still, you are watching a movie, so in that sense, some places are okay..."

• Eventually, in the end, the girl Nausicaä has to float up into the air in a striking manner.

Our contacts at Pierrot told us that summer that Kazunori Ito simply said "I'm exhausted" when he returned to the studio in the middle of the night, and then he would sit for a while with his face on his desk. (Just listening to everyone talk, our own brains would go numb.) According to Ito's calculations, if we made the first draft into a film as is, it would take nearly three years.

*

Interaction between nature and humans
Alarm bell for biotechnology
Kushana's power struggle
Pejite's independence movement
Antagonism between Nausicaä and Kushana
The miracle of green: peaceful life in the heart of the Valley of the Wind

*

Mixing the large and the small, it would be difficult to process the four or five main themes in a film that was an hour and fifty minutes (the initial estimate; in the end, it was an hour and fifty-six minutes). This was when Miyazaki's pained groans reached their peak.

The main themes above were all in the epic manga Nausicaä of the Valley of the Wind. This meant that at this time, he still was unable to distance himself from the original manga he'd been working on for a year and a half, right up until the previous month. Miyazaki himself said as much later. I suppose that even this master of filmmaking couldn't avoid falling into the pitfall of superimposing the manga on the script...

Depicting life in the valley

One thing that Miyazaki wanted to depict in the film was the way of life in the Valley of the Wind. In fact, he tried to put this in during the serialization of the manga, but at the start, he still hadn't "grasped the grammar of manga" as he said, and unable to incorporate it well, he had been forced to drop it. (He added it in when putting the chapters together for release as a book.)

"Even if it's just for one chapter, if there isn't that climax, then..." If it hadn't been for Miyazaki's sensitivity to what the fans want, the start of the second chapter of the series might have been different.

In the last scene of the first episode, Nausicaä rides *Mehve* back to the castle. Yupa follows her slowly on his Horseclaw and enters the valley—With this scene, he could draw the entrance to the valley, the area around the valley, life in the valley, the windmills, and the entrance to the castle. Perhaps a quiet scene like this would be good for the second episode of the manga… He assumed he would have the chance to draw this at some point, and then Nausicaä charged onto the battlefield.

But it would be in the film.

Going after Nausicaä, Yupa turns toward the entrance to the valley. He slips past the strange sand slats, drinks water from a reservoir pond drawn up by a windmill from five hundred meters below the ground, goes through the forest, passes the abundant fruit of the vineyards—at this time, Nausicaä is helping with repairs to the village windmills—and speaks with the kindly people of the valley.

Thanks to these few minutes, the viewer is able to see so much more. The fact that Mehve was not originally used for battle, but rather an essential part of life in the Valley of the Wind. And that the windmills are for drawing water. The fact that Yupa is respected as a human being by the people of the Valley of the Wind, etc, etc. And more than anything else, the Valley of the Wind rises up as something worth protecting.

In contrast, there were also many things that were cut because this was a movie not quite two hours long. First, Dorok does not make an appearance at all.

"They just say all this stuff that doesn't make any sense, which is why they're not in there," editor in chief Ogata noted, when pressed. But in fact, if the Tolmekian vs. Dorok plot was brought into the film, the story would end up too bloated. There was simply no way to fit it in. Also, the bloody power struggle of the Tolmekian king Vai Emperor, the princes, and the youngest princess, Kushana, is in the background of the film, but portraying it directly would have made this a different work.

At any rate, Miyazaki carved away a variety of elements from the original work and added many others.

Until the start of animation

On June 10, we moved from the former arcade and bar, the Red Room, to the renovated yakiniku restaurant that was to be the real war room. I say moved, but it was only about ten meters, so it wasn't really that much of a production.

At first, Takahata and Miyazaki were alone in this new war room, but around June 20, art director Mitsuki Nakamura joined them, and the air grew a little livelier. But given that the room was built to hold dozens of people, it still seemed pretty sad. But there was plenty of tension nonetheless, given that this was where the setting and story were steadily simmering—they were creating the floor and beams.

Ito produced a plot draft dozens of pages long based on Miyazaki's memo synopsis. If they had had more time, this would have been a springboard for discussion centering around Miyazaki, and then Ito would have written up the script. However, we absolutely had to start animating on August 1, or we might not make it in time for a March 11 theatrical release, so Miyazaki plunged straight into a rough storyboard based on his second synopsis.

At the end of July, Miyazaki had finished rough storyboards for the ABC parts of ABCD. And then he finished a clean copy of Part A before the start deadline of August 1. We still had over six months before the film would be finished, but Miyazaki had already given up his Sundays at this point.

The desk to Miyazaki's right was were Mitsuki Nakamura sat. Through meetings with Miyazaki, he'd already completed several dozen pages of concept art. His personal favorite was one of spores dancing in the forest of decay, and when it looked like this scene was going to be cut from the storyboard, he told Miyazaki, "This scene is going to be absolutely incredible. We have to leave it in." He had only met Miyazaki a couple of months earlier, but he was already perfectly in sync with his vision. The illustrator Yoshiyuki Takani, who came by to talk with Miyazaki, also praised Nakamura's concept art.

Further back in the war room was Komatsubara. He had started there a couple of weeks earlier and still seemed a little nervous. But he was a person of tremendous ability, so he was able to find his place in the team and knocked out one design after another.

The seat to the left of the entrance to the war room was occupied by Tadakatsu Yoshida of Topcraft, who had come on board at the end of July. He was the one who did the last scene of the Topcraft-produced *The Last Unicorn*, which involved a ridiculous amount of work. Miyazaki put this Yoshida in charge of the Ohm. Eventually, Yoshida moved from designing the Ohm and the insects, which were basically the same as in the manga only with fewer lines, and was put in charge of animating them, leading to him drawing over ten thousand iterations of these creatures. (Remember that massive herd at the end!)

Takahata also had a desk in the war room, but there was nothing on it. He had a video tape and a *Nausicaä* reference book, the budget, and some other things in a shoulder bag, and he went around having meetings. He was masterful in his ability to take on the unfamiliar trade of producer. When he was in the war room, he would crack jokes as if to ease the tension.

On July 29, before the start of animation, a "striking ceremony" was held at the nearby Topcraft. There, Miyazaki revealed, "If we do this right, I think it will be an 'animation' rather than a manga movie."

On July 31, we moved from the war room to the Topcraft studio, while the people doing the processing moved from the studio to the war room.

This is a bit of a tangent, but I mentioned before that at the time of *Conan* and *The Castle of Cagliostro*, Yasuo Otsuka and Miyazaki were playing kendama, for some reason. I understood the reason for that now. Fundamentally, it was a way to blow off steam. However, each time a bit of the storyboard was finished, "Will this shot go well? Yo! Ya!"

And Miyazaki would catch the ball in the cup or the hole. Soon enough, both of them got too good at this little game, so that all the shots were apparently going to go well.

With *Nausicaä*, they wagered on Tabuchi's home runs. It was a strange thing to bet on, but in May/June 1983, Seibu's Tabuchi was hitting a ton of home runs, and being a fan, Miyazaki was overjoyed. But no joy is perfect, and a pitch hit Tabuchi, putting him on the sidelines. When he heard about this, the look on Miyazaki's face was such that I wish I could show you all. He was so utterly dismayed.

"Aah, Tabuchi's used to taking a hit from the ball. He'll be back in no time," we desperately tried to console him.

In the animation trenches

August 1 was the long-awaited start of animation. We had a clean copy of the storyboard for part A. So the Topcraft staff and outsider Yukitoshi Hane got to work on animating it. Kanada and Nakamura, our own in-house animators, joined them about two weeks later.

Once animation started, all anyone did was frantically draw, so there isn't much to write about.

When you went into the Topcraft studio, the president's office was immediately to the left, with the production assistant and main staff areas beyond that. On the right was our in-house staff area with Mitsuki Nakamura, Noriko Takaya (backgrounds, machines), Kanada, Nakamura, Nabeshima, and Megumi Kagawa. Beside this was the Topcraft in-house art/video section.

Unlike the serious in-house art section, you would occasionally hear flirtatious voices from our staff area. A certain animator would surprise a woman with a toy scorpion. Of course, it wasn't all fooling around, a fact which I think those of you who have seen the film will understand.

"Hey, Miyazaki? Come look at the color of Nausicaä's eyes."

This was the color designer Michiyo Yasuda. With two cels in front of them, Miyazaki, Yasuda, and Takahata had a meeting.

"I think this one's better. Mysterious." Miyazaki chose the bright blue.

"But it's too strong. Her eyes alone will stand out? I think this is the safe choice." Takahata pointed at the slightly darker blue.

After a volley of questions and answers, Miyazaki made his decision. "Okay then, this one in general, and when she's looking closely at Teto or something, we'll go with the brighter one."

"Right." Takahata was in agreement. "When she plays with Teto, the brighter one is better."

This was also part of Miyazaki's job in between the layout and art checks.

"Wow, this is really well made." This was Kanada's voice. The plastic model gunship from Tsukuda had arrived, and Miyazaki brought it over to the art area to use as a reference for the animation. Nakamura, Nabeshima, and pioneering mech designer Mitsuki Nakamura all crowded around to see. They admiringly chimed in unison about how well-made it was.

"Still, it's probably going to be hard to draw," Miyazaki murmured, almost as though he had designed it himself, and returned to his seat. Kagawa, who was drawing a gunship scene at that very moment, slapped her hands against her desk, and everyone burst into laughter.

In August, September, and October, the key squad was struggling to create layouts (each led by key artist) on the level Miyazaki was looking for, but there was the sense that the deadline still lay ahead. There was a little room to breathe.

Miyazaki would also joke around, like when Mitsuki Nakamura brought Noriko Takaya in. "If a beautiful woman joins us, everyone will get distracted. That could be a real problem."

We had a single, middle-aged member of the editorial division sitting in at Topcraft at the time, and whenever he came back to the office, he would sigh, "I'm just so jealous of those young people." When asked why, he told us, "They're all meeting each other for the first time—like when Kagawa came from the animation studio for *Nausicaä*—but they get along with everyone right away. I'm jealous of their energy." No doubt this middle-aged editor watched them enviously while he did nothing.

In the end, *Nausicaä* was drawn by more than twenty people, but our contact was mostly limited to the staff permanently stationed at Topcraft. Which is why I can't really touch on Toshitsugu Saida and the other people from Oh!Pro or people like Yukiyoshi Hane. At best, all I have are whispers on the wind that they were working hard at Oh! Pro, saying things like, "We gotta push through on *Valley of the Wind*" and "*Valley of the Wind* rewrites?!"

Tsukasa Tannai started work as our in-house staff on November 1. I'm sure many of you know this, but Tannai had been at Telecom, where he worked on animation for *The Castle of Cagliostro*, *Sherlock Hound*, and *Lupin the Third: Farewell My Beloved Lupin*; he was a person of enormous ability. And because he was familiar with Miyazaki's style, he could do the keys at a pretty nice clip.

But we would still have to go through the pain of creation before it was all over. In the middle of December, the call to prepare for battle was finally issued, and that was the end of days off for any of the staff.

Miyazaki and his team began to spill over with tension; their hands never stopped moving, even when they were talking. Komatsubara only turned his ears to the sumo broadcast when Kitanoumi was up. Mitsuki Nakamura would trot from his seat over to Miyazaki, the two of them would both speak rapid-fire, and then he would trot back to his seat. There was also staff who silently checked the video. We were affected by this tension, as well. Even when we went to meetings for publicity or music, we were barely able to speak at all.

"Oh, you came at a good time. I'm just finishing up. Do you want to go for a drink?" Art director Mitsuki Nakamura would joke around like this and make us laugh when we still had some wiggle room in 1983. But once we got into the new year, his style changed.

"When are you *Animage* guys going to come and help us finish up?"

Naturally, any cel we painted would be a mess. But even knowing it was a joke, considering the tight spot everyone was in, we wanted to tell him that we would start tomorrow.

At the end of January, the number of keys left to do was down to twenty shots out of a total of about 1,620. You could see a little relief in the faces of the key animators, but everyone in backgrounds, in-betweens, processing, and cinematography was still tense, knowing the real fight lay ahead. The situation felt dire.

The biggest reason for this was the density of the images. For instance, to take just one background, water was added to the finished line drawing in a Sea of Decay scene, and once the ink ran, it was redrawn the same as before to bring out a depth. This was the kind of labor involved.

With the help of cinematographer Koji Shiragami and directorial assistants Takashi Tanazawa and Kazuyoshi Katayama, the team finished, after much trial and error, the elastic multi for the Ohm proposed by Miyazaki. (I wonder how many shots it took including the test filming. It was nearly enough that you could make a single anime—albeit a short one—from just the retakes. This multi was used in scenes where the Ohm is mobile.)

Or in the Giant Warrior scene, the labor and impact in the in-betweens alone is incredible, to the point where animation director Komatsubara gasped in admiration. "Aah, that's amazing. You really did a great job with this." It's not just the Giant Warrior; with scenes featuring Ohm charging, chaotic battle with people and horses, sky scenes weaving through the clouds using background in-between frames, and spores falling like snow. It's more than the amount of work put into these scenes; the level of expression in each and every place is so rich. When Nausicaä is riding Mehve, viewers can see how "flying is an expression of [Nausicaä's] feelings," as Miyazaki was always saying.

Once we had gotten this far, we were left with the nearly insurmountable issue of the final processing. The processing proved to be so difficult that even the wife of producer Isao Takahata, who was formerly processing staff at Toei Doga, pitched in.

All hands on deck

From the end of January to the beginning of February, in-house staff like Tsukasa Tannai, Osamu Nabeshima, Takashi Nakamura, Yoshinori Kanada and the other animators left the studio one after another having finished their part.

We watched over this a little sentimentally. "Aah, it's finally coming to an end." They had been camped out in the studio for a full six months, after all. It only made sense that their departure felt sad.

But when you looked at it from the overall film production, with the ending of the key animation, the studio became even more of a battleground. The in-betweens, backgrounds, cinematography, processing staff, and production assistants were transformed into fighting demons.

On February 6, we were full speed on the in-betweens. At this point in time, there were still 25,000 cels left to finish. And more than a few of these would prove difficult and require extra time. Both of the Topcraft tables were in full rotation for filming. (And of course, we were also sending work out to Takahashi Pro and other studios.) The in-house key animators who had nothing to do were conscripted as filming assistants, and the work went on twenty-four hours a day split into two shifts.

Having finished the keys for the Ohm and the insects, Tadakatsu Yoshida also moved on to processing work for the Ohms he had drawn himself. Key animator Megumi Kagawa and background's Noriko Takaya also helped with processing. While Miyazaki painted the tapestries from the opening credits on fabric in watercolor, he also helped with processing, spilling a can of paint in the midst of it. (The floor ended up completely yellow.) Takahata was in sound dubbing meetings from February 27, but he still came around the processing studio. Everyone moved around to polish the animation. Topcraft's President Toru Haru's round face even seemed haggard somehow during this time. It was precisely the situation where you look to get all hands on deck.

We sent some of those hands to the studio from our own editorial division: Manabu Nakamura, known to everyone at Animage as the one who found the good mech. For two weeks, starting on February 3, Nakamura worked hard, averaging four hours of sleep a day (in the studio). He came back to the editorial division on February 15, a dazed look on his face. When we asked him about the work, he said he prepared cans of paint during the day and helped with production checks at night. It's true he wasn't familiar with the work; nonetheless, he was practically paralyzed after a mere two weeks. We were forced to imagine the hard work of the production staff who'd been working on this for months.

And there was one more of our in-house staff left: art director Mitsuki Nakamura. Nakamura declared himself a "male Oshin," after the titular heroine of an NHK drama, and was in the studio from morning until night. He was the one creating the atmosphere, just like he had with the art, telling jokes to a roomful of people on the nervous side. He always said, "While you're all pulling all-nighters, working frantically, I'll be off by myself taking a dip in a hot spring! Ha ha ha!" but that was nothing more than a hopeful observation. Eventually, the backgrounds were in on February 23.

After his "seven months of fire" from the end of June the previous year, the amount of gray in Nakamura's hair was noticeable.

Four full days of all-nighters

We now come to the dubbing. The recording studio crammed with all kinds of machines, a myriad of knobs and switches. Just seeing all these machines, I was ready to throw my hands up in the air, but my meager knowledge grew tenfold through the experience, so I'll try to give you a general overview here.

Dubbing is the process of inserting sound to go along with the film. (Perhaps that's obvious...) This one word, "sound," encompasses so much more, roughly split up into dialogue, sound effects (FX), and music. And then each of these is split into several tracks due to varying circumstances for each, so there are a total of six or seven tapes. I forgot about this, but all of these sounds are readied in advance of the dubbing day. And it would be bad if there wasn't enough, so I'm sure they must prepare extra...

The 116-minute film *Nausicaä* is split into twelve reels, and sound is inserted into one reel (about ten minutes) at a time. First, the dialogue (the recording of which finished in the middle of February), the FX, and music prepared in advance are played as the film is shown on a screen. At this time, there's also someone fiddling with those many knobs (the mixer). There are more than seven people all together, including those in front of each of the monstrous tape players.

Miyazaki and Takahata watch to this, and then they put in orders, things like, "Take out the music," "Add in the sound of impact," or "I want to add the whooshing sound of a plane." They make all kinds of requests depending on the scene. We were concerned…what if the dubbing staff didn't have that sound?

There was also the issue of volume, apparently. They discussed and tweaked it over and over (the film playing each time they did) before they started on the finished track.

Right before the final recording, sound director Shigeharu Shiba actually sounded pretty great: "*Nausicaä of the Valley of the Wind* reel five, complete dubbing track."

And when this got to "reel twelve," it was all over. There were times when it took five tries for the finished track. This is how a single reel was finished, but they needed a minimum of four full hours to do it. The dubbing itself was supposed to be finished in four days, so they had to do a total of three reels a day. The first day, work went until eight in the morning, and then the second day started at noon, so the dubbing personnel were apparently not sleeping. In the end, that was how it was for four days.

Suguru of Suguru's *I Love Music* (Animage series) said this as well, but when they didn't have the desired sound effect there, they would take it back to the office and make it on the spot. Makes sense. Of course, this would take time.

The fifth reel was the scene Yoshinori Kanada drew of Asbel attacking the Tolmekian airship in the sky. Once the final take was finished, Shiba said to the sound personnel, "Wow! This is amazing. It's live action. It really is live action." And it's true, the scene does have incredible power. I remember that upon hearing this, one of the mixers (I think it was anyway) looked utterly delighted.

Final message

At the end of February, we were finally able to announce the end of *Nausicaä of the Valley of the Wind*, a film we'd fought tooth and nail to make since the previous May. All that was left was to wait for the release on March 11 after the first private screening on March 6 and the press screening on March 8.

Editor in chief Ogata's excitement increased in step with the approach of the release date.

"It's finally happening, hm?" we said to him.

His face flushed and he looked resolved somehow. "It is. You're right." We looked closely to see his hands were tightly clenched.

"The processing's all done, right?"

"Yes, basically a few more pages left."

"I guess you can't finish the filming first."

"Not until the processing's done."

"That so? Well, either way, it's fine."

"We managed to get it in time."

"Aah, it's really great."

He was used to deadlines with the magazine, but perhaps because he was out of his element, the string of worries knew no end.

"So someone from Toei called today. He said advance sales were good. Did you see the evening edition of the Mainichi?"

"Did they mention the advance sales?"

"A Narumi Yasuda article."

Conversations tended to be somewhat confused.

I hesitate to write about the editorial division, but during this time we were facing our own battlefield on par with that of those involved in the film production.

Work was progressing essentially simultaneously on the two volumes of *Sherlock Hound* released on February 28, the *Nausicaä Guidebook* released on March 5, the April issue of *Animage* on sale on March 10, and the *Nausicaä of the Valley of the Wind Roman Album* released on April 6. Just one book was enough to keep everyone at Animage busy, so I have no idea how we actually made all of these in that time frame.

That reminds me. I haven't touched on the publicity in these pages, but this is because we trusted Hakuhodo and the marketing department of Takahata Shoten in all ways for this major enterprise. We were not in the least bit worried in the editorial division.

They arranged for all sorts of things: billboards, TV spots, an enormous Ohm figure, an endorsement from the World Wildlife Fund. They even pulled Miyazaki into a showing of *The Castle of Cagliostro* on March 14 (*Wednesday Night Movie* on Nippon TV) and held all kinds of events.

We had our team and a divine mission… Well, that's a bit of an exaggeration, but that really was the feeling right before the theatrical release.

We went well over the initial budget and invested a vast sum into the production to create this feature-length animation *Nausicaä of the Valley of the Wind*. In the end, I wonder what kind of impact it had on the anime world—no, the film world.

✳ This text was originally serialized in *Animage* from July 1983 to April 1984 as "The Road to Nausicaä" and has been revised and edited for publication here.

CREDITS

PRESENT
Tokuma Shoten and Hakuhodo

EXECUTIVE PRODUCERS
Yasuyoshi Tokuma   Michio Kondo

ASSOCIATE EXECUTIVE PRODUCERS
Nausicaä of the Valley of Wind **Production Committee**
Tatsumi Yamashita   Tadashi Okumoto
Hideo Ogata   Hiroshi Morie

ORIGINAL STORY AND SCREENPLAY BY
Hayao Miyazaki
Based on the comic series *Nausicaä of the Valley of
Wind* in monthly magazine *Animage* published by
Tokuma Shoten.

SUPERVISING ANIMATOR
Kazuo Komatsubara

ART DIRECTION
Mitsuki Nakamura

MUSIC
Joe Hisaishi

AUDIO DIRECTOR
Shigeharu Shiba

KEY ANIMATION
Yoshinori Kanada   Tsukasa Tannai
Takashi Nakamura   Hideaki Ann
Osamu Nabejima   Megumi Kagawa
Tadakatsu Yoshida   Toshitsugu Saida
Kazuyuki Kobayashi   Tadashi Fukuda
Shuichi Ohara   Kitaro Kosaka
Takashi Watabe   Junko Ikeda
Yukiyoshi Hane   Shoji Toyama
Noboru Takano   Takanori Hayashi
Yoichi Kotabe

KEY ANIMATION ASSISTANTS
Masahiro Yoshida   Tomihiko Okubo

ANIMATION CHECK
Tadashi Ozawa   Hideo Hiratsuka

IN-BETWEEN / CLEANUP ANIMATION
Yoshiko Sasaki   Yukie Takahashi
Yumiko Taguchi   Kiyoko Saito
Kiyo Mizutani   Junko Yano
Yukari Watabe   Koji Hori
Umanosuke Iida   Daijiro Sakamoto
Kazuhisa Nagai   Yoshiko Nakamura
Yasushi Tanizawa   Taira Sanuki
Mahiro Maeda   Sachiko Tada
Yasutaka Hanafusa   Masako Kondo
Kazuhiro Ikeda

SUPPORTING ANIMATION STUDIOS
Oh!Production   Studio Pokke
Kusama Art   Hadashi Pro
AGU   Doga Kobo
Studio Toto   Studio 501
Studio Aton   Random
Yamato Pro

BACKGROUND
Kazuhiro Kinoshita   Toshio Nozaki
Masaki Yoshizaki   Kuniko Nishimura
Kazuo Ebisawa   Studio Bic
Design Office Mecaman   Satoshi Miura
Tatsuo Aoki   Tokuo Okazaki
Yuko Sugiyama   Kazuo Okada
Kimiko Shimono   Ritsuo Imamura
Tetsuto Shimono   Keiko Togashi
Hiroko Murai   Kaoru Chiba
Miyoshi Takanami

HARMONY TREATMENT
Noriko Takaya

COLOR DESIGN
Michiyo Yasuda   Fukuo Suzuki

INK AND PAINT CHECK
Homi Ogiwara

INK AND PAINT
Taeko Omi   Emiko Ishii
Yumi Furuya   Wakako Sugano
Hiromi Nagamine   Chiharu Mizuma
Makiko Yamauchi   Masayo Yoshida
Richiko Shimizu   Tomohiro Yamamuro

SUPPORTING INK AND PAINT STUDIOS
Easy World   ProStudio Robin
Hokusai   Hadashi Pro
Shinsei Pro   Yuminsha
Studio 2001   Studio Hibari
Studio Marine   Yamato Pro

CAMERA
Takashi Shirakami   Yukiasa Shudo
Yasuhiro Shimizu   Mamoru Sugiura

CAMERA SUPPORT
Takahashi Production   Masao Miyauchi
Akio Hirayama   Takeo Kobayashi
Anime Friend   Studio 35

TITLE
Takagu Atelier

EDITING
Tomoko Kida   Naoki Kaneko
Shoji Sakai

SOUND EFFECTS
Noriyoshi Ohira   Kazutoshi Sato

ASSISTANTS TO THE DIRECTOR
Takashi Tanazawa   Kazuyoshi Katayama

PRODUCTION MANAGERS
Sumi Sakai   Shigehiro Suzuki

PRODUCTION ASSISTANTS
Naoyuki Oshikiri   Mamoru Kanbe
Nanako Shimazaki

ADVERTISING PRODUCER
Masaya Tokuyama

AUDIO RECORDING
Omnibus Promotion

RECORDING AND SOUND MIXING
Kunio Kuwabara

RECORDING STUDIO
Shinsaka Studio

FILM DEVELOPING
Toei Chemical Industry

"Nausicaä of the Valley of the Wind"
PRODUCTION COMMITEE
Tokuma Shoten   Hakuhodo
Yutaka Wada   Takashi Sato
Kenji Ohara   Kentaro Nakatani
Toshio Suzuki   Shiro Miyazaki
Osamu Kameyama   Tsutomu Otsuka

PRODUCTION
Top Craft   Toru Hara

DISTRIBUTION
Toei Company, Ltd.

PRODUCER
Isao Takahata

DIRECTOR
Hayao Miyazaki

THEME SONG
"Kaze no tani no Nausicaä"
LYRICS   Takashi Matsumoto
MUSIC   Haruomi Hosono
PERFORMANCE   Narumi Yasuda
                (Tokuma Japan)

VOICES
Nausicaä: Sumi Shimamoto
Jihl: Masato Tsujimura
Obaba: Naoko Kyoda
Yupa: Goro Naya
Mito: Ichiro Nagai
Gol: Kohei Miyauchi
Gikkuri: Joji Yanami
Niga: Minoru Yada
Girl C/Toeto: Rihoko Yoshida
Girl A: Masako Sugaya
Girl B: Takako Sasuga
Boy A: Chika Sakamoto
Boy B: TARAKO
Asbel: Yoji Matsuda
Lastel: Mina Tominaga
Pejite Mayor: Makoto Terada
Lastel's Mother: Akiko Tsuboi
Kushana: Yoshiko Sakakibara
Kurotowa: Iemasa Kayumi
Commander A: Tetsuo Mizutori
Pejite Citizen: Takemi Nakamura
Pejite Girl: Takako Ota
Pejite Citizen: Satoshi Shimada
Tolmekian Soldier: Shinji Nomura
Boy: Hisako Ayuhara
Tolmekian Soldier: Yoshitada Otsuka

THE ART OF
NAUSICAÄ
──OF THE VALLEY OF THE WIND──

Based on the Studio Ghibli Film

Original Story and Screenplay Written and Directed
by **Hayao Miyazaki**

English Adaptation/Jocelyne Allen
Design & Layout /Yukiko Whitley
Design Assistant/Natalie Chen
Copy Editor/Justin Hoeger
Editor/Nick Mamatas
Sr. Director, Publishing Production/Masumi Washington

© 1984 Studio Ghibli
First published in Japan by Tokuma Shoten Co., Ltd.

Printed in China

Published by VIZ Media, LLC
P.O. Box 77010
San Francisco, CA 94107

First printing, April 2019

Visit www.viz.com